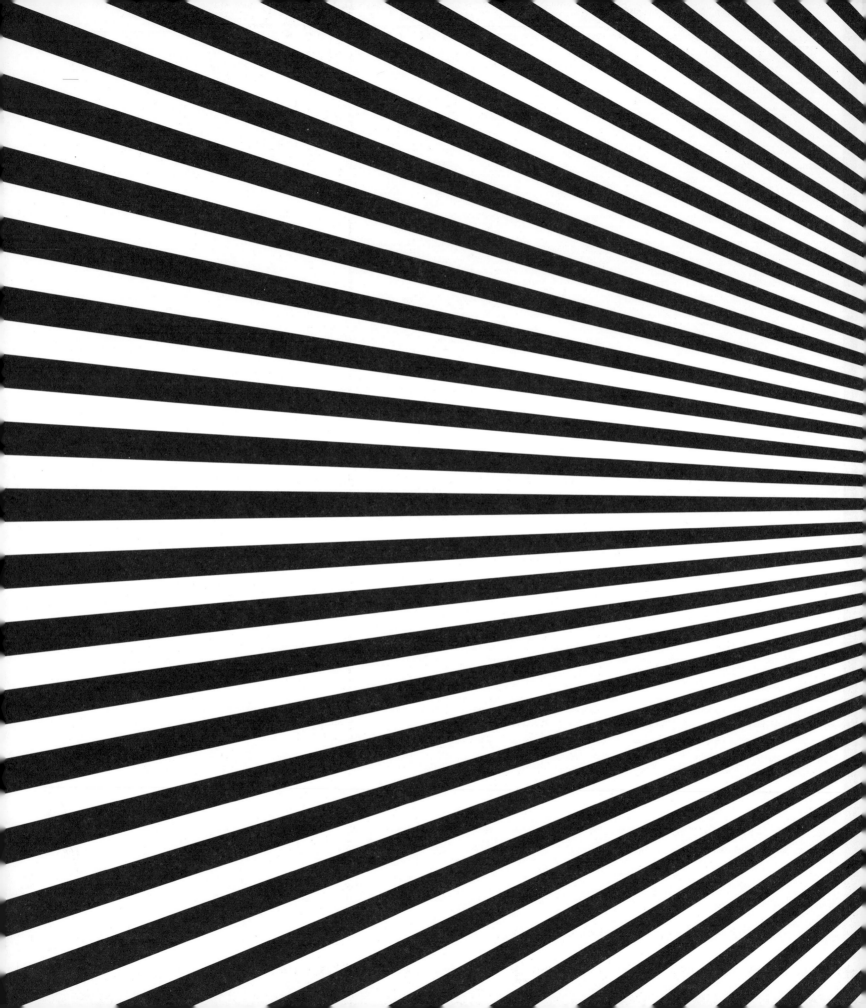

SFJAZZ

SFJAZZ

THE FIRST 30 YEARS

SETTING THE STAGE

ISBN 978-14521-19861

Manufactured in the United States of America

Design by Public
Text by Susan Wels

10 9 8 7 6 5 4 3 2 1

Chronicle Books LLC
680 Second Street
San Francisco, CA 94107
www.chroniclebooks.com/custom

Photo Credits

Drew Altizer pg. 122; Bengston pgs. 62, 68 upper right; Jay Blakesberg pg. 91; Mark Brady pgs. 7, 74, 101, 119; Mars Breslow pgs. 58, 60, 98, 109 left and center; Stuart Brinin pgs. 13, 18, 26, 28–29, 35 upper left, 39, 41, 42, 44, 45, 47, 50, 51, 52, 53, 54, 55, 57, 63, 64, 65, 68 upper left, 70; Clayton Call pg. 118; Matt Campbell pgs. 80, 117 upper right; Mark Cavagnero Associates pgs. 124–125, 127, 128, 130–131; Tim Charles pgs. 110, 111; Scott Chernis pgs. 67, 92, 95, 97 upper left, 98, 99, 108, 110, 114; Tom Copi pgs. 25, 26; D. Darr pg. 59; Ronald Davis pgs. 100, 104; Walt Denson pgs. 102, 106, 116, 117 upper left, 120; Deanne Fitzmaurice pg. 26; Davis Ibarra pg. 93; Bonnie Kamin pgs. 8, 22, 24; Marty Kelly pg. 33; James Knox pg. 107; Sun Lee pgs. 78, 81, 88, 94, 95, 103, 108, 109 right, 116, 118; Terry Lorant pgs. 14, 21; Maiden pg. 65; Richard Mayer pg. 16; Steve Mundinger pg. 66; Michael Piazza pgs. 40, 46, 56, 69 upper right, 73, 79, 96, 108; James Radke pg. 48; Susan Ragan pgs. 17, 36; Jerry Stoll pgs. 84, 85; Stuart Schwartz pgs. 61, 134–135; Marty Sohl pgs. 12, 14–15; J Thackray pg. 77; Greg Toland pg. 112; Gerry Waitz pgs. 30, 34, 38; Lewis Watts pg. 69 upper left

Table of Contents

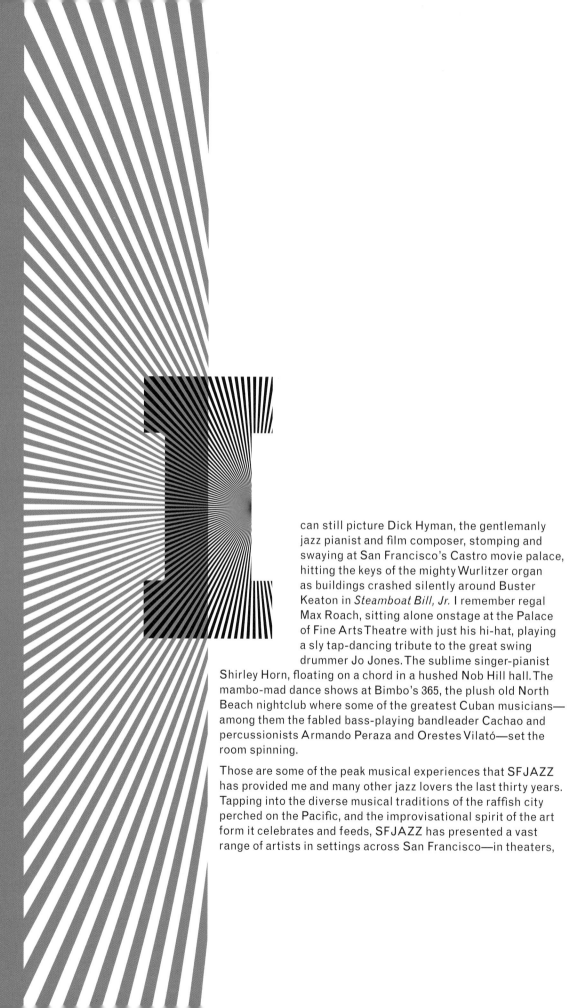

can still picture Dick Hyman, the gentlemanly jazz pianist and film composer, stomping and swaying at San Francisco's Castro movie palace, hitting the keys of the mighty Wurlitzer organ as buildings crashed silently around Buster Keaton in *Steamboat Bill, Jr.* I remember regal Max Roach, sitting alone onstage at the Palace of Fine Arts Theatre with just his hi-hat, playing a sly tap-dancing tribute to the great swing drummer Jo Jones. The sublime singer-pianist Shirley Horn, floating on a chord in a hushed Nob Hill hall. The mambo-mad dance shows at Bimbo's 365, the plush old North Beach nightclub where some of the greatest Cuban musicians— among them the fabled bass-playing bandleader Cachao and percussionists Armando Peraza and Orestes Vilató—set the room spinning.

Those are some of the peak musical experiences that SFJAZZ has provided me and many other jazz lovers the last thirty years. Tapping into the diverse musical traditions of the raffish city perched on the Pacific, and the improvisational spirit of the art form it celebrates and feeds, SFJAZZ has presented a vast range of artists in settings across San Francisco—in theaters, clubs, and cathedrals, at sunset on the bay, in the streets at midnight—that suited the music and gave the San Francisco Jazz Festival its cosmopolitan flavor.

The provocative clarinetist Don Byron played comic Mickey Katz klezmer at Temple Emanu-El. The late tenor saxophone master Joe Henderson strolled through the Gothic arches of Grace Cathedral, riffing off his echo and Indian percussion wizard Zakir Hussain, who summoned the sound of rain and fluttering bird wings. Across the street at the Masonic Auditorium, João Gilberto, the whispering voice of bossa nova, sat hunched over his guitar in the spotlight, singing sensuously sad and beautiful songs, one after another, without saying a word.

Some of those artists, as well as younger stars like Joshua Redman and Esperanza Spalding, appear in the pages of this lively book, which tells the story of SFJAZZ, an organization that brought forth a bounty of memorable music during the last three decades. From it's early days as Jazz in the City—a grassroots enterprise that evolved from a two-day, money-losing festival into one of the world's premier jazz presenters—SFJAZZ specialized in thematic programming that hit the right notes in a town with wide tastes in jazz, blues, Latin, and experimental music. And it built fresh programs around the great artists living in the Bay Area: Peraza, Vilató, Hutcherson, and Hussain; drummers Tony Williams and Eddie Marshall; singers Bobby McFerrin and Mary Stallings; singer-songwriter Dan Hicks; the Kronos Quartet.

Under the leadership of cofounder Randall Kline, a perfectionist with an ear for quality and the ambition to build a major arts institution from the ground up, SFJAZZ has always been about putting good music of many kinds onstage, and seeding the future of jazz by commissioning new music from leading artists and nurturing young talent in its bands and classroom programs. In addition to producing commissioned pieces by musicians as varied as Anthony Braxton, Redman, and Williams (who played his piece at the Herbst Theatre with Kronos, his blazing quartet, and the deep Mr. Hutcherson), Kline has crafted original programs that introduced audiences to mesmerizing tap

dancers—the flying Nicholas Brothers, hummingbird bird–like Bunny Briggs, the slammin' Savion Glover—and major works like Duke Ellington's 1965 *A Sacred Concert*. Composed for and performed by Ellington at the consecration of Grace Cathedral, the concert, which featured such stirring performers as gospel singers Esther Morrow and Jimmy McPhail, alto saxophonist Johnny Hodges, and the above-mentioned Briggs (gliding across the cathedral floor as the band played a soft, snapping version of Ellington's "Come Sunday" set to "And David Danced Before the Lord" from the biblical book of Samuel). SFJAZZ re-created the piece on the twenty-fifth anniversary of its inaugural performance, with Briggs, McPhail, and the Ellington Orchestra, led by Duke's son, Mercer, merging with the Oakland Interfaith Gospel Choir to praise the Lord in Duke's sacred and swinging language.

Not everything has worked. But Kline and his colleagues—and the funders, sponsors, donors, musicians, and fans who've embraced the endeavor—have always been game to think big and take a chance on something that could turn out to be great.

That adventurous spirit, so central to jazz and San Francisco, has found expression in the SFJAZZ Collective, a hothouse for new music by some of the most creative artists on the scene, and the new SFJAZZ Center, the country's first stand-alone building conceived and designed solely for jazz. Set in the bustling heart of San Francisco's Hayes Valley, down the block from the San Francisco Symphony, Opera, and Ballet, the luminous structure designed by architect Mark Cavagnero promises to be not only a splendid place to play and hear music, but a vital part of the neighborhood, the city, and the global evolution of jazz. Who knows what jazz will sound like in thirty years, but now it's got a permanent home in San Francisco, where the music can be made new again, night after night.

ABOVE

Vibraphonist Bobby Hutcherson at the Palace of Fine Arts Theatre, performing with McCoy Tyner, in 2009.

JAZZ
IN
THE

Chapter One

1983–1989

CITY

AZZ IS ABOUT RISK—mixing it up, creating, and improvising in real time. It's also about mastery, passion, and collaboration. With skill and a spirit of invention, magic can happen.

Thirty years ago, two young music promoters, Randall Kline and his business partner Clinton Gilbert, rolled the dice on a new idea—an urban jazz festival that would showcase the immense talent and diversity of Bay Area artists. San Francisco had always been a mecca for jazz. Ragtime and blues fueled the heyday of the Barbary Coast. "Jelly Roll" Morton—the self-proclaimed inventor of jazz—lived there in 1923, and Lu Watters sparked the city's traditional jazz revival in the 1940s. In the '50s, San Francisco drew modern jazz innovators like Charles Mingus, Miles Davis, John Coltrane, Dave Brubeck, Gerry Mulligan, Chet Baker, and Cal Tjader, and in the early '80s, the city was full of world-class artists. Great local talent included vibists Bobby Hutcherson and Monk Montgomery; saxophonists Joe Henderson, Pharoah Sanders, John Handy, Mel Martin, and Stan Getz; drummers Tony Williams, Eddie Moore, and Eddie Marshall; singers Mary Stallings and Bobby McFerrin; pianists George Cables and Denny Zeitlin; and Latin percussionists John Santos, Armando Peraza, Orestes Vilató, and Pete Escovedo. San Francisco also had a wealth of unique venues and an arts-loving, savvy, adventurous public.

Kline and Gilbert wanted to try something new to expand the audience for the rich, free-spirited jazz scene in San Francisco. Other jazz festivals tended to showcase specific genres, but none offered the wide variety of jazz that flourished in the city's multicultural environment. San Francisco was famous for risk-taking and experimentation, and Kline and Gilbert wanted to present its vibrant jazz scene in all its glory, from Afro-Caribbean music and African drumming to the avant-garde.

They took their idea to Kary Schulman, who headed the city's Hotel Tax Fund/Grants for the Arts program. "They were young, scruffy guys with great energy and great ideas," Schulman recalled, "so I said, 'Show us what you can do.'" With $20,000 in grants from the Hotel Tax Fund and the San Francisco Foundation—a huge sum in those days for upstart presenters—Kline and Gilbert launched the inaugural Jazz in the City Festival in June 1983. The two-day event, held at Herbst Theatre, featured an eclectic, all–Bay Area lineup including the Afro-Cuban group Orquesta Batachanga; Mel Martin's Bebop and Beyond; stride pianist Mike Lipskin, the avant-garde Now! Artet; and vocalists Nicholas, Glover, and Wray, a trio inspired by the Boswell Sisters of the 1930s.

The festival was not a success. The house was half full each night, execution was rough, and the event lost money. Many presenters would have chosen to throw in the towel and move on. But the music was great—there was no doubt about that. Kline and Gilbert, and their funders, believed that they should try again.

Focusing on fundamentals

It wasn't hard to figure out why the first festival didn't work. A diverse lineup can succeed in an outdoor setting, where patrons can chat or walk around if they don't like a band. But in a concert hall, with no distractions, it can be hard for a wide-ranging program to hold an audience; some listeners might love Latin jazz, but they may not be fans of bebop or avant-garde. So Kline and Gilbert decided to focus each show around a single, niche style of jazz that could highlight the depth of Bay Area talent and attract the audience that was most interested in that style. The Hotel Tax Fund and the San Francisco Foundation provided grant money for the second festival. A nonprofit consortium, the Arts Loan Fund of Northern California, loaned the presenters funds to cover the previous year's loss. Kline and Gilbert moved the event to October, establishing a new fall jazz tradition, and they copresented it with the Asian-American Jazz Festival to use resources more efficiently.

The five-day 1984 Jazz in the City headlined the masterful duo of George Cables and Bobby Hutcherson, solo vocalist Bobby McFerrin, the Rova Saxophone Quartet, and others. That year, the festival's Youth in Jazz program debuted. The concert, recognizing great young players, featured the nationally renowned Berkeley High School Jazz Ensemble with a talented teenage tenor saxophonist, Joshua Redman.

This time, everything came together. Jazz in the City took off. The festival was an artistic and fiscal success, and Kline and Gilbert were able to meet all their financial commitments. During the next five years they kept taking risks while focusing on business fundamentals.

Kline was going to as many events and venues as he could to gauge what was working and what wasn't. When he went to a screening of a film about jazz and saw the packed house, he realized there was a way to expand jazz's reach in the city while generating more cash for the festival. In 1985 he and Gilbert launched the first Jazz in the City Film Festival at the Roxie Theater, presenting movies, documentaries, and programs by jazz archivists. In 1988, the event featured a new film, *That Rhythm, Those Blues*, about R&B singer Ruth Brown and pianist Charles Brown, whose intimate vocal stylings had influenced Ray Charles. Brown, then sixty-six and living in a Bay Area senior-housing facility, performed several of his hits on the theater's upright piano. "It was a great and moving moment," Kline said, "to hear the legendary Charles Brown playing so beautifully in such a humble setting." The performance marked the beginning of a comeback for Brown.

Vocalist Bobby McFerrin headlined a 1984 concert of solos and duos in the Green Room at the War Memorial Performing Arts Center.

Pianist and vocalist Charles Brown performed at his seventy–fifth birthday salute at Oakland's Paramount Theatre in 1997.

The Rova Saxophone Quartet onstage at the First Unitarian Church in 1984

AT AGE FIFTEEN, TENOR SAXOPHONIST JOSHUA REDMAN made his Jazz in the City debut, playing with Berkeley High School's legendary jazz band at the first Youth in Jazz concert. Three years later, Redman graduated first in his class from Berkeley High. He went on to Harvard, graduating summa cum laude and Phi Beta Kappa, and had already been accepted at Yale Law School when he changed his plans.

Although he had never thought of music as a career, Redman had always kept playing the saxophone—in his college band, with friends from Boston's Berklee School of Music, and doing occasional gigs as a college senior. The son of free-jazz saxophonist Dewey Redman and dancer Renee Shedroff, he had grown up immersed in global musical styles and traditions, from classical, jazz, rock, and hip-hop to gamelan. In 1991, instead of going to New Haven, he went to New York to hone his jazz skills on the tenor sax. That November, he entered and won the Thelonious

Monk International Jazz Saxophone Competition. Part of the prize was a recording contract with Warner Bros., so Redman decided to delay law school and see what happened. He was an instant phenomenon.

Two years later, when Redman was twenty-four, his first album earned him a Grammy nomination. He also opened the 1993 San Francisco Jazz Festival—returning to its stage not as a student but as an internationally acclaimed star in a powerhouse quartet with Pat Metheny, Billy Higgins, and Christian McBride. By the end of the decade, Redman had won first-place finishes in the *Rolling Stone* critics' poll, the *Jazziz* readers' poll, and *Down Beat*'s critics' and readers' polls. As Peter Watrous of the *New York Times* observed, "There's only a handful of naturally gifted musicians, and Joshua's one of them. Every time you hear him, he's at a higher level."

Redman moved back to the Bay Area in the 1990s and, ever since, he's had a great

collaboration with SFJAZZ. In 2000, he became artistic director of its new Spring Season, and from 2004 to 2007, he served as founding artistic director of the SFJAZZ Collective. Now living in Berkeley with his wife and children, Redman continues to record and perform frequently.

"It's rare and gratifying to watch a star-is-born story unfold," said Randall Kline. "Joshua's aesthetic, his broad view of jazz, is a great fit with ours. He's a great partner." He's also, according to *Down Beat*, "perhaps the most influential jazz artist of his generation."

OPPOSITE
In 1993, Redman opened the San Francisco Jazz Festival, playing with Pat Metheny (on guitar) and Christian McBride.

1984

YOUTH IN JAZZ STAR
JOSHUA REDMAN

JOE HENDERSON was a prolific composer and one of the most influential tenor saxophone players in jazz history. He had a distinguished career, recording five albums as a leader and countless other records for the Blue Note label in the 1960s. Henderson played with Herbie Hancock, Miles Davis, and Blood Sweat & Tears. But by time he moved to San Francisco in 1971, rock 'n' roll was eclipsing jazz, and Henderson was performing, touring, and teaching with a lower profile than he'd had in his heyday as a jazz heavyweight.

In 1985, at age fifty-eight, Henderson played in the third annual Jazz in the City Festival, sharing the stage with Orestes Vilató as guest stars with John Santos's Afro-Cuban Jazz Ensemble. The next year, Randall Kline asked him if he'd do a duet concert, in the fourth festival, with a talented eighteen-year-old double bassist named Larry Grenadier. A Bay Area native, Grenadier had already been playing with professional musicians for a couple of years, and he and his brothers—Phil, a trumpeter, and Steve, a guitarist—had performed in the 1985 Jazz in the City Festival. He was still in his teens and about to enter Stanford University, but he was playing jazz at a professional level.

Henderson was always up for something new, and he agreed. His duet with Grenadier would be staged in the Green Room of the downtown War Memorial building. An hour before the show was supposed to start, however, Henderson still hadn't shown up, so Kline called him at his home in San Francisco's Forest Hills neighborhood. Henderson answered the phone and explained that he had already driven down to the War Memorial—half an hour away—but he couldn't find anywhere to park, so he'd gone home. Kline immediately offered to send somebody to pick him up, and Henderson got to the Green Room with minutes to spare.

He and Grenadier had never met before, and they hadn't even discussed what they would play.

ABOVE
Henderson, a fifty-eight-year-old saxophone star, and Grenadier, a talented eighteen-year-old double bassist, performed a spectacular, spur-of-the-moment duet in the War Memorial's Green Room in 1986.

OPPOSITE
Henderson starred with the Joe Henderson Band in the 1993 "We Love Joe" tribute concert at Davies Symphony Hall.

1986

JOE HENDERSON AND LARRY GRENADIER

While Kline introduced them to the audience, Henderson quietly explained to the young bassist how they would play the intro to "Recorda Me," the Latin jazz standard Henderson had written in 1963. The two artists, Kline recalled, then proceeded to perform one of the greatest concerts that he's ever heard.

It was an amazing moment, and Henderson went on to enjoy a career renaissance. In the early 1990s, he was signed to the Verve label and recorded a series of albums that earned Henderson four Grammies, including Best Album and Best Instrumental Solo. In 1992, Henderson also won *Down Beat* magazine's triple crown—for Album, Tenor Saxophonist, and Jazz Musician of the Year. He won those honors in both the *Down Beat* international critics' and readers' polls, making him a double triple crown winner— the only one in history besides Dizzy Gillespie.

He was an incomparable artist and a star again, and to celebrate him, the San Francisco Jazz

Festival staged a "We Love Joe" concert in 1993. Grenadier—who is now considered one of the top bassists in the country—continued to perform with Henderson, touring with his band in the 1990s, as well as with jazz masters Stan Getz, Gary Burton, singer Betty Carter, and pianist Brad Mehldau.

Pushing the boundaries

Jazz in the City also started commissioning new pieces. In 1986 it premiered *Composition No. 132* by jazz-maverick saxophonist Anthony Braxton, who was teaching at Mills College in Oakland. Funded in part by the National Endowment for the Arts, the work debuted in the soaring Gothic spaces of Grace Cathedral. The avant-garde spectacle included two orchestras—led by Braxton and a second conductor, communicating by headset—as well as modern dancers on separate stages and roving soprano saxophonists wearing silver space suits.

That same year, Jazz in the City introduced its Jazz Masters Series, celebrating historically significant jazz artists and eras. In 1988 it staged a rollicking Stride Piano Summit, bringing together piano virtuosos Dick Hyman, Ralph Sutton, Jay McShann, and Mike Lipskin—along with trumpeter Harry "Sweets" Edison—at a show that packed Davies Symphony Hall. The next year, it took dynamic jazz performance to a new level. Its two-day Jazz Tap Summit featured living tap legends Charles "Honi" Coles, the Nicholas Brothers—the famous Cotton Club performers and Hollywood film stars—and "Sandman" Sims, the incomparable tap master of Harlem's Apollo Theater.

Jazz in the City was stretching the definition of jazz, preserving jazz traditions, and expanding its audience and community. From gospel and East/West fusion to Afro-Caribbean styles, its shows reflected the diversity of San Francisco, in spaces selected to enhance the music. At the Palace of Fine Arts Theatre, Davies Symphony Hall, the Palace of the Legion of Honor, Grace Cathedral, Bimbo's 365 Club, and boats on the bay, Jazz in the City took a nomadic, adventurous approach, creating thoughtful mixes of music and venues.

OPPOSITE

In 1986 composer and saxophonist Anthony Braxton debuted his *Composition No. 132*, the first Jazz in the City commission, in the towering, vaulted spaces of Grace Cathedral.

IN 1988 THE SAN FRANCISCO JAZZ FESTIVAL commissioned a new work by composer, pianist, drummer, and tenor saxophonist Peter Apfelbaum. Then twenty-eight years old, he was already one of the great talents in jazz. Born and raised in Berkeley, California, Apfelbaum had played with the award-winning Berkeley High School Jazz Ensemble and had formed his own seventeen-piece orchestra, The Hieroglyphics Ensemble, before he graduated.

Apfelbaum wove global, nontraditional musical forms into extraordinary jazz-fusion compositions. "My vocabulary," he wrote, "reflects the fact that I started life as a drummer, was trained in jazz theory, blues, and gospel music as a pre-teenager, became absorbed in African and Latin music as a teenager, listened to a lot of contemporary classical music, worked in R&B, reggae, blues, Latin, African, jazz, funk, Middle Eastern, and Indian bands, and, for as long as I can remember, I've been fascinated by how sounds can be fitted together."

For the premiere of his festival commission, *Notes from the Rosetta Stone*, Apfelbaum asked legendary trumpeter Don Cherry to be his guest soloist. Cherry, fifty-two, had already been charting new musical territory for thirty years. An adventurous, avant-garde artist, he started playing and recording with Ornette Coleman in the 1950s and went on to perform with John Coltrane and Sonny Rollins. In the 1970s, Cherry began exploring world fusion, studying Indian, African, and Middle Eastern music and instruments. He was a free spirit and his sound, on the pocket trumpet and cornet, was hard to categorize. "What I learned to do," he said, "was look at the horn, know what it was supposed to sound like, and then go for a new tone that could take me and the audience into a fresh place." Cherry was a jazz pioneer, geomusical explorer, conceptual artist, and inspirational teacher.

He agreed to play with Apfelbaum at the Jazz in the City concert. It was a fateful match. Cherry liked the Bay Area so much that he moved to San Francisco from New York City. He formed a new group, Multikulti, with Apfelbaum and two players from The Hieroglyphics, and they toured all over the world for the next two years. Cherry also performed frequently with The Hieroglyphics, and he premiered his own Jazz in the City–commissioned work in a 1989 Grace Cathedral concert featuring Apfelbaum and Brazilian percussionist Nana Vasconcelos.

A year after Cherry died, in 1996, Apfelbaum dedicated an album to his longtime collaborator. He also performed in the 1996 San Francisco Jazz Festival's "Tribute to Don Cherry" concert at Grace Cathedral, with Vasconcelos, tenor saxophonist Dewey Redman, and double bassist Charlie Haden.

1988

When legendary trumpeter Don Cherry (pictured) performed with composer, drummer, pianist, and saxophonist Peter Apfelbaum for the first time at the Palace of Fine Arts Theatre in 1988, the two jazz greats launched a long-term collaboration.

DON CHERRY AND PETER APFELBAUM

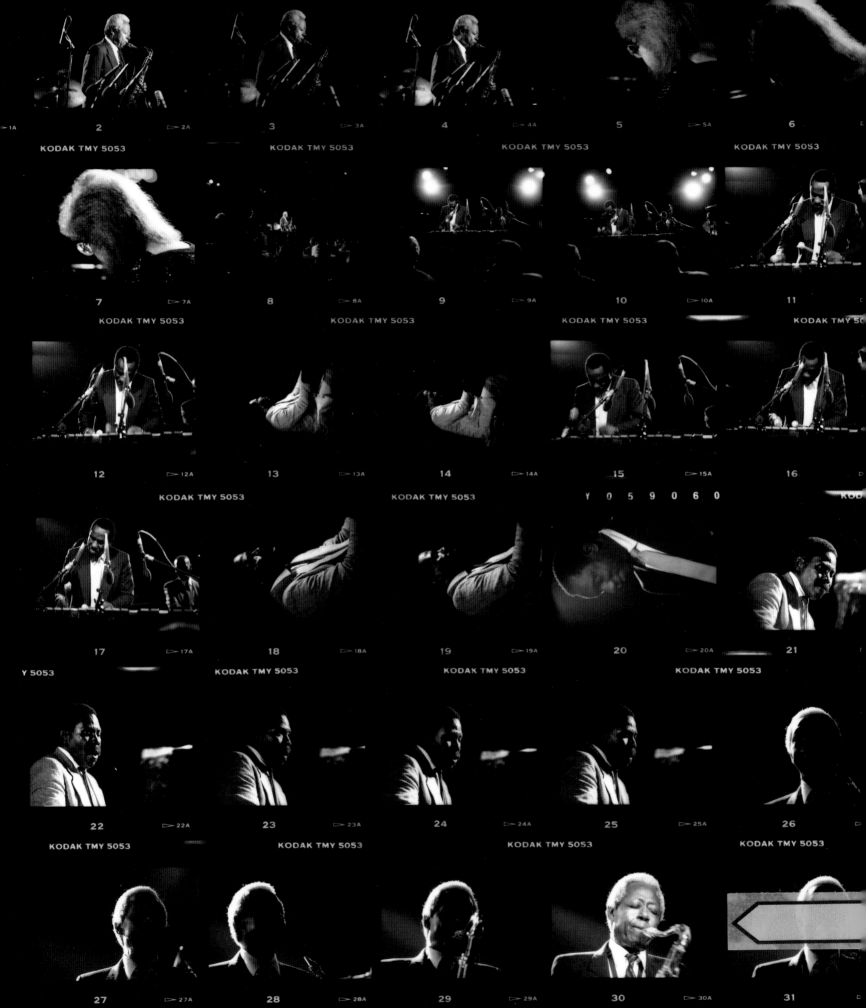

The "Thelonious Monk Birthday Tribute" in 1988 featured (far left, top to bottom) Charlie Rouse, Jessica Williams, Buddy Montgomery, and George Cables; the 1989 Jazz Tap Summit at Davies Symphony Hall starred (bottom row, left to right) Harold and Fayard Nicholas, Steve Condos, and Eddie Brown.

Behind the scenes, Kline and Gilbert were building a jazz institution from the ground up. They looked to the San Francisco Symphony as a great model. It had first-class performance, education and audience-development programs, and financial stability when other symphonies were struggling. Jazz was being called America's classical music, so why couldn't jazz have a similar cultural profile in San Francisco?

Jazz in the City was expanding quickly. It was launching its own educational programs for youths and adults and working successfully with a wide range of funders and sponsors. Kline and Gilbert were thinking like an institution long before their annual festival became one. In discussions with their funders, they mentioned the idea of someday having a facility of their own. "That's a great idea," said Francesca Gardner, grant officer for the James Irvine Foundation. "Put it out there—you never know."

With their fiscal know-how and spontaneous, creative, think-on-your-feet working style, they were producing a music event that was getting noticed. In 1989, the *San Francisco Chronicle*'s jazz critic, Jesse Hamlin, wrote that "It's rare to find a jazz festival that actually takes chances in the spirit of the risky art it's celebrating. While the big festivals tend to rehash predictable formulas, San Francisco's Jazz in the City sticks its neck out a little farther each year."

The Nicholas Brothers at the 1989 Jazz Tap Summit

SAN
FRANCISCO
JAZZ
FESTIVAL

Chapter Two

1990–1999

**AN FRANCISCO WAS JAZZ CITY IN THE 1990s.
Americans were tuning in to world culture,
and jazz, with its global roots, had a growing
audience. San Francisco, especially, embraced
eclectic, multicultural jazz styles and hosted
what was becoming the most acclaimed jazz
festival in the country.**

Jazz in the City, declared *Jazz Times*, was "well
on its way to world-class status." With its rising
national profile, it adopted a new name—the San
Francisco Jazz Festival. It was attracting critical
praise, it was fearless, and it was growing fast.

In early 1990, the San Francisco Jazz Festival
staged an ambitious spectacle. On April 29—the
birthday of the late Duke Ellington—it presented
the twenty-fifth anniversary of the Duke's
majestic *Concert of Sacred Music*, a work that he called "the
most important thing I have ever done." The anniversary event,
funded by a grant from the Hewlett Foundation, re-created the
work's 1965 premiere at Grace Cathedral. The historic concert
featured the Duke Ellington Orchestra, directed by Ellington's
son, Mercer; the Oakland Interfaith Gospel Choir; the gospel
soloist who sang at the premiere, Jimmy McPhail; the tap dancer
from the first performance, Bunny Briggs; and narrator and jazz
soloist Brock Peters, who was featured in the original recording.
Both performances at the cathedral were sellouts.

"A DRUMMER LIKE TONY [WILLIAMS] COMES ALONG ONLY ONCE IN THIRTY YEARS," Miles Davis said. A child prodigy, Williams was born in Chicago, raised in Boston, and started playing drums when he was eight years old. He was soon playing professionally, and, at seventeen, he joined Miles Davis's quintet, with pianist Herbie Hancock, bassist Ron Carter, and saxophonist Wayne Shorter. That band became one of the most influential and produced some of the greatest recordings in jazz history. It is hard to overstate Miles Davis's admiration for Williams. The drummer was, he said, "the center that the group revolved around."

In 1969 Williams, who recorded for Blue Note, formed his own pioneering group, The Tony Williams Lifetime. That seminal ensemble—featuring guitarist John McLaughlin, former Cream bassist Jack Bruce, and organist Larry Young—created a heavy-duty fusion of jazz, R&B, and rock. Over the years, Williams kept pushing the envelope as a drummer, improviser, and composer with an aggressive, unpredictable sound that's been described as "controlled chaos."

Eventually Williams, who lived in the Bay Area, returned to the acoustic jazz genre, composing and forming a band with some of the country's best young players. In 1987 he headlined at Jazz in the City, and in 1990—recognizing Williams's creative legacy and the great band he sustained—the festival commissioned him to write a new work. That year, the San Francisco Jazz Festival premiered Williams's composition—for string quartet, jazz drums, cymbals, and piano—as the centerpiece of a dream-concert celebration called "The Music of Tony Williams." The one-of-a-kind performance featured the Williams Quintet, the Kronos Quartet, and an electric trio featuring Williams with Herbie Hancock on the keyboard and Alphonso Johnson on the electric bass.

"Tony Williams was a dynamo," said Randall Kline. "He was the most exciting drummer to watch," and the show was historic—"one of the best evenings in concert jazz," wrote the *San Francisco Examiner*, that "we've heard during eight years of [San Francisco Jazz Festival] presentations."

Legendary drummer and composer Tony Williams (right) rehearsed his new work, a San Francisco Jazz Festival commission, with Herbie Hancock (left) before its premiere at Herbst Theatre in 1990.

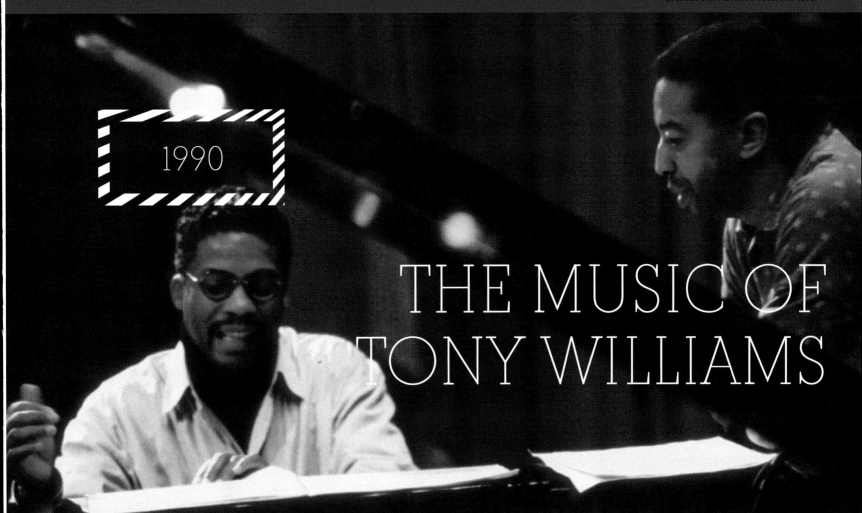

1990

THE MUSIC OF TONY WILLIAMS

The next spring, the San Francisco Jazz Festival presented the world premiere of Charles Mingus's posthumous magnum opus, *Epitaph*, and a range of national acts, including a Boogie Woogie Piano Summit—featuring Charles Brown and others—as well as two nights of tap greats at Davies Symphony Hall and a solo piano Cecil Taylor concert at Grace Cathedral. It was an outstanding lineup, but the numbers, in the end, didn't pencil out. Ticket sales for some concerts were disappointing, and the San Francisco Jazz Festival had a significant deficit. Its part-time staff and resources were overstressed. So the organization regrouped.

In 1992, it staged no spring performances, instead consolidating them into an ambitiously large-scale San Francisco Jazz Festival. The expanded seventeen-day extravaganza was a big roll of the dice, but it paid off. Fifty-thousand people packed twenty-two events featuring jazz legends and rising stars, including Tony Bennett; Mario Bauzá, inventor of the mambo; Elvin Jones, Pharoah Sanders, and Tommy Flanagan in a John Coltrane tribute; Clarence Fountain and the Blind Boys of Alabama; guitarist Bill Frisell; Benny Carter's big band; singers Mary Stallings and Madeline Eastman; and a historic Indian music and jazz experiment by alto saxophonist John Handy and sarod master Ali Akbar Khan, with Zakir Hussain. By focusing on a large San Francisco Jazz Festival, the organization efficiently leveraged its small staff and advertising budget, setting the stage for a decade of explosive growth.

Cecil Taylor in a solo performance at Grace Cathedral in 1991

OPPOSITE

Bill Frisell at the Palace of Fine Arts Theatre in 2001; Zakir Hussain (center) with Ustad Alla Rakha in the 1996 "Percussion Maestros of North and South India" show at Masonic Auditorium, featuring Pharoah Sanders

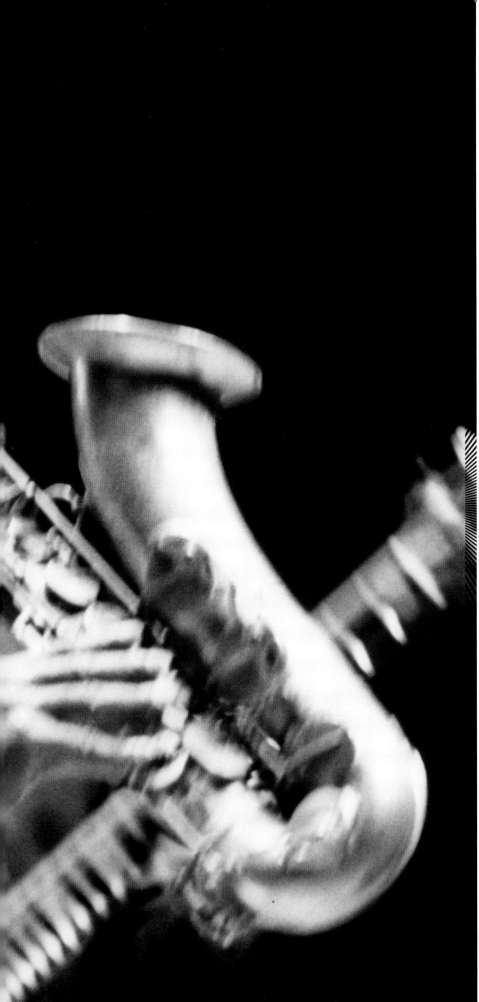

Taking chances

In 1993 the festival revisited its roots. Young tenor saxophone sensation Joshua Redman, who had played in the first Youth in Jazz concert, returned and opened the festival as an acclaimed star. The lineup also featured daredevil clarinetist Don Byron playing a concert of klezmer music, as well as a rousing "We Love Joe" show celebrating master saxophonist Joe Henderson's "rediscovery," along with his new Grammy-winning albums on the Verve label.

LEFT

**Joe Henderson with John Scofield
at the 1993 "We Love Joe" concert at
Davies Symphony Hall**

The San Francisco Jazz Festival reflected the best of the national jazz scene and the unique, adventurous Bay Area jazz culture. Festival director Randall Kline liked to include "wild cards" to keep things interesting, and San Francisco audiences continued to take chances. One of the festival's most memorable and historic performances was the 1994 premiere of *Tone Dialing* by avant-garde jazz pioneer Ornette Coleman. The multimedia work combined the debut of Coleman's acoustic quartet, featuring pianist Geri Allen, with spoken word, video effects, and a live, onstage demonstration of body piercing by Fakir Musafar.

Dizzy Gillespie in 1991 at Herbst Theatre with the Dizzy Gillespie Big Band

Ornette Coleman premiered his avant-garde composition *Tone Dialing* at Masonic Auditorium in 1994.

ONE EVENING IN 1994, Randall Kline was riding his bike home from the San Francisco Jazz Festival loft on 10th Street, as he did each night. It was a Tuesday, around 8 p.m., and as he biked across Market Street and up Grant Avenue, he heard the wail of an alto saxophone.

"The sound was notably great," Kline said, "much better than any street musician I'd ever heard." As he biked past Post Street, he spotted the sax player standing on a deserted corner. It was no one he knew, but the sound was so compelling that Kline turned around, rode back, got off his bike, and sat down on the sidewalk to listen to him play for half an hour.

Afterward, as light was fading, Kline got up and introduced himself to the musician. "I asked him his name, and he told me that he was Sonny Simmons," Kline said. "I was amazed. Simmons was a great musician, a legend." In the 1960s, he'd been a leading free-jazz artist in New York City, playing with Sonny Rollins, Don Cherry, Charles Moffat, Eric Dolphy, and other masters.

But Simmons had hit hard times, starting in the 1970s. After he moved to California with his wife, jazz trumpeter Barbara Donald, and their young son, financial and family pressures stalled his music career. Simmons put his sax in the garage, and it stayed there for years, covered with cobwebs and dust, while he hustled for jobs. Eventually, Simmons turned to alcohol and drugs. His marriage crumbled, and he ended up homeless in San Francisco, playing his music for change on the streets for more than a decade.

"It was crazy to run into him like that," Kline said. The sax player stayed on his mind, and a few weeks later, Kline asked Branford Marsalis how he'd feel about having Simmons open his upcoming show at Masonic Auditorium. "Branford loved the idea," Kline said, "and he told me he'd always been a fan of Sonny Simmons." Their concert in the packed, three-thousand-seat hall was "fantastic," Kline said, and Simmons played beautifully.

That year, the saxophonist's life started to change. Other fans rediscovered him, too, and Sonny Simmons was able to resurrect his career. Since then, he has appeared in festivals and clubs around the world; launched a new group, the Cosmosomatics; and recorded eleven new albums as a leader. In 2008, Simmons received a Lifetime Achievement Award from the American Jazz Foundation.

1994

SONNY SIMMONS

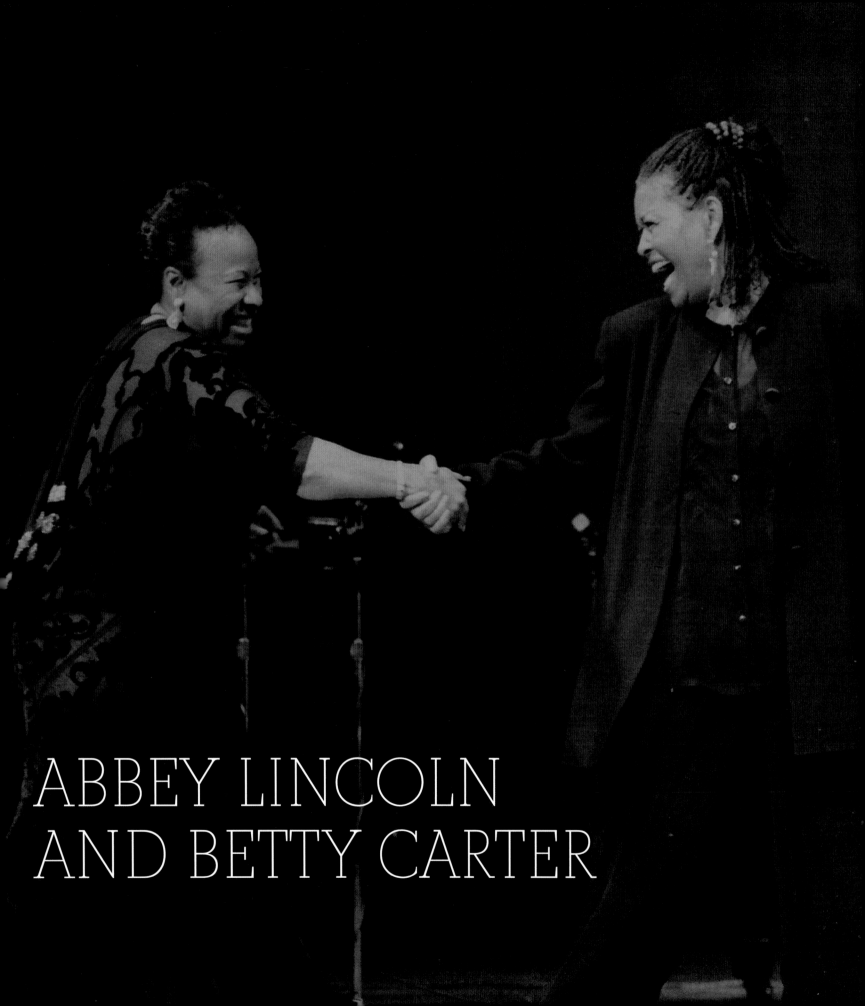

ABBEY LINCOLN
AND BETTY CARTER

1994

WHEN TWO GREAT JAZZ
SINGERS, ABBEY LINCOLN
AND BETTY CARTER, teamed up
on a double bill for the first time
in the 1994 San Francisco Jazz
Festival, it was a rare moment. The
legendary vocalists, the same age,
were both Grammy winners, Verve
recording stars, and uncompromis-
ing individuals.

Lincoln's vocals and compositions were poetic, dramatic, and
deeply expressive. An actor and
committed civil rights activist, she
had performed with jazz greats
including Max Roach, Sonny
Rollins, Stan Getz, and Bobby
Hutcherson.

Betty Carter was famous for
her unique improvisational style,
dazzling range, and inventive, pas-
sionate scat singing. She was also
known for her tough personality.
A demanding performer—whose
band was considered a "finish-
ing school" for talented young
players—Carter had been a vocalist
with Lionel Hampton, Charles
Mingus, Wes Montgomery, and
Ray Charles. She had also started
her own record label in 1969
and staged a comeback in 1979
with her self-produced album
The Audience with Betty Carter,
recorded at San Francisco's Great
American Music Hall. Carter had
real staying power—she had been
voted Number One Female Jazz
Singer in *Down Beat*'s critics' and
readers' polls every year
since 1989.

Since Verve was a sponsor
of the jazz festival, it seemed like
a natural to feature Carter and
Lincoln with their bands in a
double bill. The two vocalists had
never sung together, and at their
concert in the three-thousand-seat
Masonic Auditorium, they
almost didn't.

Lincoln performed with her
band during the first half, then
waited backstage while Carter
sang with her own powerhouse
band in the second set. They
were supposed to close the show
with a duet, but Carter, lost in the
moment, was having a great set
and didn't call Lincoln back to
the stage. Carter's set was going
much longer than it was supposed to, and Lincoln was pretty
sure the duet wouldn't happen.
She wanted to leave, but emcee
Billy Dee Williams courageously
strode onto the stage when Carter
finished a song, took the mike, and
called Lincoln back up for the final
number. The two legends, in the
spotlight together, hugged each
other, stood arm in arm, and sang
a stunning, show-stopping duet
that brought down the house.

**Masterful vocalists Betty Carter
(left) and Abbey Lincoln, shown
here with Dave Holland, performed
together for the first time at the
Great American Music Hall in 1994.**

Latin percussionist
Armando Peraza in the 1995
"Tribute to Armando Peraza"
show at Masonic Auditorium

WHEN THE 1994 SAN FRANCISCO JAZZ FESTIVAL opened with Dave Brubeck and Gerry Mulligan at Davies Symphony Hall, it was a rare San Francisco reunion of two legendary West Coast jazz pioneers.

In the late 1940s, Mulligan arranged and played baritone saxophone with Miles Davis's nonet, which became a leader of the cool jazz sound. When Mulligan moved west to Los Angeles in 1952, the historic quartet he formed with Chet Baker became synonymous with West Coast jazz. Mulligan often came up to San Francisco to play gigs at the Black Hawk nightclub—home base to composer and pianist Dave Brubeck's quartet, renowned for its own West Coast jazz innovations.

From 1968 to 1972, the two jazz giants teamed up as "The Dave Brubeck Quartet with Gerry Mulligan." In 1994 they hadn't played together in years, and their performance at the San Francisco Jazz Festival—together and with their own bands—was an emotional, unforgettable replay of jazz history.

West Coast jazz pioneers Dave Brubeck and Gerry Mulligan reunited in 1994 at Davies Symphony Hall.

1994

DAVE BRUBECK AND GERRY MULLIGAN

Dave Ellis and Charlie Hunter at the
1995 11th Street Block Party

Rising jazz star Diana Krall opened for legendary pianist George Shearing in 1996 at Masonic Auditorium.

THE 1996 SAN FRANCISCO JAZZ FESTIVAL scored a coup when pianist George Shearing made it the initial date on his first quintet tour since the 1970s. Opening for him at the festival that year was another pianist—a relatively unknown jazz artist named Diana Krall. It was obvious to everyone listening that night that Krall—with her cool, intimate vocals and soulful piano style— could carry an entire concert of her own.

Krall, a British Columbia native, had been singing and playing with a trio in New York City. In 1993 she had released her debut album on a small, independent Canadian label, and her second CD had gotten good reviews. In 1996, her third album—a tribute to Nat King Cole—rocketed to the top of the charts, earning her a Grammy nomination, and it stayed in the top ten listings for two years.

In 1998, Krall returned to the San Francisco Jazz Festival as a rising superstar. She has since won three Grammy awards and recorded nine gold, three platinum, and seven multiplatinum albums.

1996

DIANA KRALL

The 1995 festival's 11th Street Block Party, a club-hopping/street party in the city's newly hip SoMa district, showcased the city's new acid jazz scene. And in 1996 a new, unknown jazz talent, Diana Krall, opened for pianist George Shearing in a festival that also headlined Sonny Rollins and Asian-American jazz artists like kotoist Miya Masaoka and tablaist Zakir Hussain. The San Francisco Jazz Festival was, in the view of the *New York Times*, "possibly the country's best," and the *Chicago Tribune* called it "the crown jewel of American jazz festivals." America's cultural center of gravity was moving west, the *Tribune* proclaimed, and the San Francisco Jazz Festival was one reason why. It was, the paper declared, "unrivaled as the most intelligently programmed and creatively staged jazz soiree in America."

Organist Jimmy Smith played with saxophonist Red Holloway and hard-bop guitarist Mark Whitfield at the 1995 11th Street Block Party.

ABOVE

**Wayne Shorter in 1995 with bass
guitarist Christian McBride,
drummer Will Calhoun, and the
Wayne Shorter Electric Band, at
Masonic Auditorium**

OPPOSITE

**Sonny Rollins in 1999 at Masonic
Auditorium**

FOLLOWING SPREAD, FROM LEFT

**Max Roach in a 1996 solo performance at the Palace of Fine Arts Theatre;
Dee Dee Bridgewater in 1996 at Herbst Theatre**

John Lee Hooker in 1996 at Oakland's Paramount Theatre; Bonnie Raitt,
Ruth Brown, and "Little" Jimmy Scott in 1997 at the "Charles Brown 75th Birthday"
concert; Joe Williams and Nancy Wilson in 1997 at Masonic Auditorium; John Hendrix and
Cassandra Wilson in the 1997 performance of Winton Marsalis's Pulitzer Prize–winning
***Blood on the Fields*, with the Jazz at Lincoln Center Orchestra, at Masonic Auditorium**

FOLLOWING SPREAD, FROM LEFT
**Ruben Gonzalez in 1998 at Davies Symphony Hall; Roy Haynes in 2005 in his
eightieth-birthday show at Masonic Auditorium**

Celia Cruz in the 1997 "Salsa Dance Party"
at Bill Graham Civic Auditorium

Charles Lloyd and Billy Higgins
in the 1997 "Drum Summit" at
Masonic Auditorium, featuring
the Elvin Jones Jazz Machine and
Roy Haynes Group

PREVIOUS SPREAD, FROM LEFT
**Marc Anthony starred in the 1998 "Salsa Dance Party" and "Fiesta Boricua"
at Bill Graham Civic Auditorium.**

ABOVE

**Israel "Cachao" Lopez headlined
in "La Evolución de la Música Afro-
Cubana" at Davies Symphony Hall.**

OPPOSITE

**Paco de Lucía starred in the 1996
"Three Guitars" show with
Al Di Meola and John McLaughlin.**

**Master of the *laúd*, or Cuban lute,
Barbarito Torres headlined in
a 2000 show at Yerba Buena Center
for the Arts.**

**Michael Ray and the Cosmic Krew in the 1996 Halloween show at the
Palace of Fine Arts Theatre; Tito Puente at the 1999 "Salsa Dance Party"
at Bill Graham Civic Auditorium**

Jazz trumpeter Ambrose Akinmusire has been blowing away audiences since he was at Berkeley High School. A member of its jazz ensemble—one of the country's top incubators for jazz talent—he performed with the band at the San Francisco Jazz Festival in 1999.

After winning a full scholarship and studying at the Manhattan School of Music, Akinmusire did postgraduate work at the Thelonious Monk Institute of Jazz Performance at the University of Southern California. In 2007, he entered and won the Thelonious Monk Instrumental Jazz Competition, dazzling a panel including Quincy Jones, Terence Blanchard, Clark Terry, and Roy Hargrove with his phenomenal horn playing. That year, Akinmusire also won top honors at the prestigious Carmine Caruso International Jazz Trumpet Solo Competition.

Since then he has burst onto the jazz scene with his riveting tone, expressive style, and creative vision. Akinmusire has worked with artists including Herbie Hancock, Wayne Shorter, Ron Carter, Jimmy Heath, Jason Moran, and Esperanza Spalding. In 2011 his debut Blue Note album, *When the Heart Emerges Glistening*, won critical praise. Akinmusire, who has led his own groups at two SFJAZZ events, is more than a great trumpet player, according to Herb Alpert, "he's an artist."

Akinmusire, winner of the Thelonious Monk Instrumental Jazz Competition, first performed in the San Francisco Jazz Festival in 1999, when he was in high school.

1999

YOUTH IN JAZZ STAR AMBROSE AKINMUSIRE

Planning the future

Cofounder Clinton Gilbert had left the organization, and Randall Kline was now steering its development and operations. Thanks to its high performance level and small, dedicated staff, it was blooming into an urban jazz institution. With city, state, federal, corporate, private, and foundation funding and a budget that had burgeoned to $3 million, the organization was staging a first-class San Francisco Jazz Festival and almost a hundred shows a year, including free outdoor lunchtime concerts in the summer. It was also developing new audiences for jazz through free in-school concerts; "Kids' Night Out" tickets for Bay Area students; Youth in Jazz concerts showcasing young, local talents; and discussions and demonstrations for adult listeners. Working with National Endowment for the Arts organizational development programs and a team of management consultants, it was focusing on good business practices and strategic planning. It was also taking advantage of opportunities.

LEFT

San Francisco Jazz Festival education programs included family matinees with artists including vocalist Faye Carol (top) and drummer Howard Wiley.

Don Pullen in 1994 at Herbst Theatre; Keith Jarrett in 1999 at the Opera House; Gonzalo Rubalcaba in 1997 at Herbst Theatre; and Chucho Valdés in 1998 at Davies Symphony Hall

When one of its sponsors, Embarcadero Center, offered free office space, the San Francisco Jazz Festival moved out of its 10th Street loft, south of Market, and into the office tower complex at Embarcadero Center, on the city's waterfront. And when the *San Francisco Chronicle* published a pullout advertising section in the Sunday newspaper's weekly magazine, the San Francisco Jazz Festival was suddenly reaching eight hundred thousand subscribers in the Bay Area. The pullout section continued for six years. The festival was also getting free airtime from local TV stations for public service spots produced by Goodby, Silverstein & Partners and Butler, Shine, Stern & Partners, San Francisco's top advertising agencies.

The San Francisco Jazz Festival organization was also starting to explore the possibility of its own facility. "We were always overreaching," Kline explained. "We were small, scruffy, and resourceful, and we frequently attempted to accomplish improbable things."

By the end of the decade—a time when jazz clubs were struggling and digital technology was transforming the music industry—the organization was still doubling its budget every year or two and expanding, once again, into year-round programming. By celebrating the jazz tradition—its history and acknowledged masters—as well as global, cutting-edge styles, the San Francisco Jazz Festival was continuing to grow the audience for live jazz performance.

OPPOSITE
Vocalist Etta James in 2000 at
Davies Symphony Hall

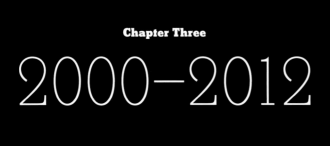

Chapter Three

2000–2012

JAZZ WAS IN TRANSITION IN THE EARLY TWENTY-
**FIRST CENTURY. Performing and recording
opportunities were getting scarcer across the country,
but San Francisco had a growing appetite for jazz.
Bay Area audiences were moved and inspired by the
action of live jazz performance, and they wanted
more jazz programming, more often.**

So the San Francisco Jazz Festival took another leap,
rebranding and reinventing itself as a year-round
presenter. It changed its organizational name to SFJAZZ
and introduced an expansive spring program of concerts,
films, and educational programs.

The new SFJAZZ Spring Season started strong, from
March through June 2000, with five weekends of performances by multigenerational, multicultural jazz greats.
Programmed by Randall Kline and tenor saxophone
star Joshua Redman—the Spring Season's new artistic director—the
concerts explored jazz's wide variety of genres and cultural styles and
its living, breathing "Tradition in Transition," as Redman titled the
second Spring Season lineup.

LEFT
**Hermeto Pascoal in 2002 at the
Palace of Fine Arts Theatre**

OPPOSITE
**Cesária Évora in 2000
at Masonic Auditorium**

ABOVE, FROM LEFT

Wynton Marsalis with the Jazz at Lincoln Center Orchestra in 2011 at Davies Symphony Hall; Ray Brown in 2001 at Herbst Theatre

OPPOSITE, FROM LEFT

Saxophonist David Murray, pianist Jon Jang, and drummer Eddie Marshall performed the world premiere of Jang's "Up from the Root" at Herbst Theatre in 2002.

**João Gilberto in 2003
at Masonic Auditorium**

ABOVE, FROM LEFT
**Caetano Veloso at Masonic Auditorium in 2007; Merle Haggard in
the "Salute to Bob Wills" show at Masonic Auditorium in 2002**

FOLLOWING SPREAD, FROM LEFT
**Herbie Hancock, Michael Brecker, and Roy Hargrove in 2002 at
Masonic Auditorium; drummer Stanton Moore with Chris Wood at the
Regency Ballroom in 2002**

Elvin Jones and McCoy Tyner at the 2002 "John Coltrane Tribute Concert" at
Masonic Auditorium; pianist Alice Coltrane in her last public performance,
at Masonic Auditorium in 2006

OPPOSITE

Ahmad Jamal, with Idris
Muhammad on drums and James
Cammack on bass, at Herbst
Theatre in 2005

SFJAZZ

It was a turning point, and SFJAZZ was finding its rhythm. Four years later, SFJAZZ took another calculated risk to push jazz forward and reflect its growth as an institution. In 2004 it launched the SFJAZZ Collective, a collaborative, visionary, resident octet. The original ensemble comprised Redman, its artistic director; legendary vibraphonist Bobby Hutcherson; trumpeter Nicholas Payton; drummer Brian Blade; pianist Renee Rosnes; bassist Robert Hurst; trombonist Josh Roseman; and alto saxophonist Miguel Zenón.

Funded by a $300,000 grant from the James Irvine Foundation, the SFJAZZ Collective is a band unlike any other in jazz. The ensemble has tremendous freedom and a two-part mission—to create new music and interpretations of works by modern jazz masters. Each year, all members of the group—composers as well as top musicians in jazz—are commissioned to write new works for the Collective. Then, in intensive multiweek rehearsals, they also workshop eight new arrangements of pieces by seminal contemporary composers—including Ornette Coleman in the ensemble's first year, followed by John Coltrane, Herbie Hancock, and Thelonious Monk. Grammy-winning jazz pianist and producer Gil Goldstein was the octet's arranger for the first three years. The group also leads educational workshops and performs in the Bay Area and on the road. The *New York Times* called the birth of the Collective "a Eureka moment in jazz." In 2006 it was voted Rising Star Jazz Group by the critics' poll of *Down Beat* magazine, and in 2007 it was named Jazz Ensemble of the Year by the Jazz Journalists Association.

"The Collective was an experiment that went right," Kline said. "We did good research and a lot of hard work, with good intentions, to produce the highest-quality ensemble and bring the SFJAZZ Collective to life. By moving music forward and celebrating jazz as a dynamic tradition, the Collective embodies SFJAZZ's organizational philosophy."

The second **SFJAZZ** Collective, in 2005, included (center, clockwise from left) **Nicholas Payton**, **Bobby Hutcherson**, **Joshua Redman**, and **Renee Rosnes**, as well as **Matt Penman**, **Eric Harland**, and **Miguel Zenón**.

San Francisco middle school students explore the connections between jazz and other subjects in SFJAZZ's free "Jazz in the Middle" program for public schools.

Expanding its reach

SFJAZZ was also nurturing the next generation. In 2001 the organization created the SFJAZZ High School All-Stars, a big band providing advanced jazz training and performance opportunities to the best young jazz musicians from all over the Bay Area. The ensemble's musicianship was so high that, in its first year, it was a national finalist in Jazz at Lincoln Center's High School Jazz Band competition. SFJAZZ also debuted new programs in public middle schools, bringing internationally renowned stars and Bay Area masters into auditoriums and classrooms.

Its new "Jazz in the Middle" program began offering free artist teaching residencies that were closely linked to the middle-school curriculum. The program helped students build their literacy by exploring the connections between jazz and poetry, history, and other academic subjects. Family matinees, at bargain prices, featured major artists, and appreciation classes, listening parties, and in-depth discussions gave adults a chance to learn more about jazz music and its history.

SFJAZZ was widening and deepening its outreach. In 2001 it held a three-day symposium—"Jazz and Race: Black, White and Beyond"—that probed the historic and contemporary relationship of race and the evolution of jazz. In 2002 it staged another in-depth exploration of a cultural issue—"Jazz Women"—which featured a panel discussion by experts on jazz and gender. More than a thousand people participated in each program, increasing the dialogue about jazz, its history, and its possibilities.

The spoken word and other forms of creative expression were becoming part of the expanding aesthetic expression of SFJAZZ. The 2003 SFJAZZ Spring Season featured the word jazz of Ken Nordine, the music-infused poetry of Sekou Sundiata, and the unique pairing of California Poet Laureate Quincy Troupe and expressive alto jazz saxophonist Oliver Lake. SFJAZZ was also honoring artists in an array of disciplines. In 2000 drummer Eddie Marshall received the first SFJAZZ Beacon Award, which celebrated Bay Area musicians for their contributions to the local jazz scene. In 2012 SFJAZZ chose poet, playwright, novelist, and essayist Ishmael Reed as its first Poet Laureate and Jim Goldberg as its first Photographer Laureate. "Their aesthetics have the same palette as ours," Kline explained. "Jazz is at the center of what we do, and SFJAZZ supports expression that resonates across all the art forms."

In 2002, activist Angela Davis and composer/percussionist Susie Ibarra took part in an SFJAZZ symposium on "Women and Jazz" at Masonic Auditorium.

Eartha Kitt in 2006 at Masonic Auditorium; Marisa Monte at the Palace of Fine Arts Theatre in 2006

2000–2012

ABOVE, FROM LEFT

**Shirley Horn at Masonic Auditorium in 2005; Yusef Lateef at Grace Cathedral
in 1998**

Madeleine Peyroux in 2005 at the Palace of Fine Arts Theatre;
Julian Lage at Herbst Theatre in 2006

**Sam Rivers in 2004 at Herbst Theatre; Joe Zawinul in 2006 at the
Palace of Fine Arts Theatre; Lou Donaldson, with Dr. Lonnie Smith
on organ, at the Palace of Fine Arts Theatre in 2008; James Cotton
in 2006 at Herbst Theatre; drummer Jack DeJohnette, with Don Byron,
at Herbst Theatre in 2008**

Tap dancer Savion Glover at the
Palace of Fine Arts Theatre in 2009

Composer and pianist Hiromi at
Herbst Theatre in 2009

Ledisi at the Palace of Fine Arts
Theatre in 2010

RICHARD BONA AND LIONEL LOUEKE

RICHARD BONA WAS BORN AND RAISED IN MINTE, IN CENTRAL CAMEROON. A musical prodigy, he built his own twelve-string guitar out of wood and bicycle brake cables. He discovered jazz and the electric bass as a teenager, inspired by the intricate, expressive innovations of Weather Report's Jaco Pastorius. Bona went to Europe to study music at age twenty-two, and in the mid-1990s, he moved to New York, where his extraordinary virtuosity on the electric bass led to collaborations with Harry Belafonte, Paul Simon, Harry Connick Jr., Chaka Khan, Queen Latifah, Bobby McFerrin, Tito Puente, Pat Metheny, George Benson, and Herbie Hancock.

Lionel Loueke grew up listening to traditional music and playing percussion and guitar in the West African nation of Benin. After studying classical music history in Ivory Coast, he went to Paris to study jazz, then won a scholarship to Boston's Berklee School of Music. Two years later, Loueke auditioned before Herbie Hancock, Wayne Shorter, and Terence Blanchard to earn a place at the Thelonious Monk Institute of Jazz in Los Angeles. Hancock "flipped," he said, at Loueke's fearless guitar playing. "It was as though there was no territory that was forbidden." Since then, Loueke has worked with artists including Hancock, Cassandra Wilson, Wayne Shorter, Charlie Hayden, and Sting.

In a rare pairing, Loueke and Bona blended their global, genre-blurring virtuosity into a joyful, mesmerizing Spring Season performance at Yerba Buena Center for the Arts. The two artists melded their African rhythms, pristine voices, and multicultural musicality into a jazz idiom and a new, heart-achingly beautiful sound.

Lionel Loueke (left), from Benin, and Richard Bona, from Cameroon, performed a rare duet concert at Yerba Buena Center for the Arts in 2009.

2009

THE ROOTS

MIXING HIP-HOP WITH JAZZ, FUNK, ROCK, AND RAP, The Roots brought a sold-out Davies Symphony Hall audience to its feet in a boisterous performance that broke through the boundaries of jazz.

The charismatic, Grammy-winning band marched down to the stage playing percussion instruments to the thundering blasts of a tuba. Remixing and rearranging their own material and classics by Black Sabbath, Guns N' Roses, and Donna Summer, The Roots gave a roaring performance, the first hip-hop show in the symphonic venue.

The group—famous as the house band for *Late Night with Jimmy Fallon*—has its roots in Philadelphia jazz. Bandleader Ahmir "Questlove" Thompson spent his high school years in Philadelphia listening to Max Roach, Tony Williams, and other seminal jazz drummers, and the band has a deep understanding of what came before. Jazz is a big tent, and San Francisco, according to Questlove, is one of those places that fosters artists who cross cultures and genres. "San Fran," Thompson said, "has always stayed excited about the music."

The Grammy-winning band The Roots—featuring rapper Black Thought (left) and sousaphonist Damon "Tuba" Gooding Jr.—staged the first hip-hop performance at Davies Symphony Hall in 2009.

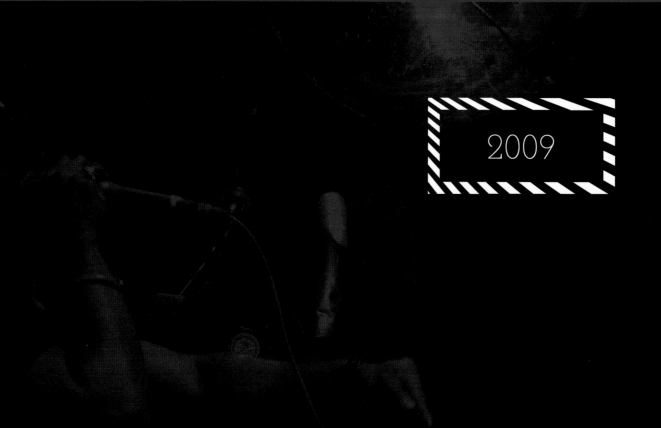

2009

IDENTICAL TWINS REMY AND PASCAL LE BOEUF grew up in Santa Cruz and played in the SFJAZZ High School All-Stars in 2003 and 2004. Now twenty-six, the Le Boeuf Brothers have racked up a string of national and international honors, including Independent Music Awards for Best Album and Best Song, twelve ASCAP Young Composer Awards, and first place in the International Songwriting Competition.

Pascal, a pianist, and Remy, an alto saxophonist and clarinetist, have won critical acclaim for their modern-jazz compositions infused with indie rock, chamber music, and electronics.

Their latest album, *In Praise of Shadows*, took jazz recording to a new digital level, inviting listeners to manipulate the tracks on their own computers.

The brothers, now based in New York, are part of a new wave of provocative, progressive young jazz artists. "It's just great to watch them evolve as players," said Dee Spencer, who directed them in the SFJAZZ High School All-Stars. They are "brothers in musical crime and creative invention," according to *Down Beat*, with "chops and a flexible pocket of ideas" about where jazz could go in the next decade. The Le Boeuf Brothers have performed at the Monterey Jazz Festival, Umbria Jazz Festival, Montreal Jazz Festival, the Kennedy Center, Carnegie Hall, and Jazz at Lincoln Center.

Remy Le Boeuf (on saxophone) and his twin brother Pascal (on keyboard) played in the SFJAZZ High School All-Stars and have won Independent Music awards for Best Album and Best Song.

2009

YOUTH IN JAZZ STARS: THE LE BOEUF BROTHERS

**Rosanne Cash and John Leventhal at Herbst Theatre in 2010; Kurt Elling,
with the Count Basie Orchestra, in the 2010 "Sinatra, Basie and More" concert
at Davies Symphony Hall**

ABOVE, FROM LEFT

Booker T. Jones at Herbst Theatre in 2010; Vijay Iyer at Yerba Buena Center for the Arts in 2010; Brad Mehldau in 2007 at Herbst Theatre; Herbie Hancock in 2007 at Masonic Auditorium; Andrew Hill at Herbst Theatre in 2006; and Jason Moran at Herbst Theatre in 2004

Dorado Schmitt at the 2011 Django Reinhardt Festival at Herbst Theatre;
Keb' Mo' and **Taj Mahal** at Masonic Auditorium in 2008; and **Marc Ribot**
accompanying Charlie Chaplin's silent film *The Kid*, at Yerba Buena Center
for the Arts in 2011

ABOVE, FROM LEFT

Kenny Barron (left) and Mulgrew Miller in a duet concert at Herbst Theatre in 2012; Maria Schneider conducted the Maria Schneider Orchestra, with Ingrid Jensen on the trumpet, at Herbst Theatre in 2002

SFJAZZ
SPRING
SEASON

PREVIOUS SPREAD, FROM LEFT

"A Night in Treme," at Davies Symphony Hall in 2011, featured Donald Harrison on saxophone, Kermit Ruffins on trumpet, Big Sam on trombone, Dr. Michael White on clarinet, and the Rebirth Brass Band; Esperanza Spalding at Davies in 2010

Brazilian singer-songwriter Céu at Herbst Theatre in 2009; Belgian
harmonica master Toots Thielemans at Herbst Theatre in 2004; "soul queen"
Irma Thomas at the Palace of Fine Arts Theatre in 2011; and Brazilian
singer Carlinhos Brown at Masonic Auditorium in 2007

A world of music

Meanwhile, the San Francisco Jazz Festival was more ambitious than ever. Its wide-angled view of music encompassed a huge range of styles, points of view, and places of origin, including Africa, Europe, South America, the Middle East, India, and the Bay Area. The Festival was presenting adventurous jazz-related, globally inspired music, from the fierce bass lines and luminous English, Spanish, and Portuguese vocals of Esperanza Spalding to the transcendent, dissonant harmonies of Le Mystère des Voix Bulgares and the classical Indian artistry of Ravi and Anoushka Shankar. It was also throwing more curveballs—including a joyful tribute to Western swing legend Bob Wills, starring Merle Haggard, and an electric fortieth anniversary performance of John Coltrane's *Ascension*, his masterwork of structured improvisation, by the Rova Saxophone Quartet and guest stars. SFJAZZ was eclectic, wide ranging, and unpredictable—and "the #1 jazz festival in the world," according to the *London Observer*.

OPPOSITE, FROM TOP

The Bulgarian Women's Choir at Grace Cathedral in 2008; Ladysmith Black Mambazo at Herbst Theatre in 2007

ABOVE

Ravi Shankar at Davies Symphony Hall in 2011

In the middle of a tough economy, SFJAZZ was having record success by focusing on the fundamentals of great music and a great listening experience. It faced occasional deficits and the constant challenge of shifting audience tastes and habits, but it continued to grow. By 2010, it had two codirectors—Randall Kline and Felice Swapp. It also had a full-time professional staff, active board members and contributors, an endowment fund, and an expanding membership base of more than three thousand people. SFJAZZ was also, finally, beginning to build its first permanent home. With a $25 million anonymous gift and $10 million from its board, the organization was embarking on a $63 million project to create the space that it had envisioned for almost thirty years.

In 2011 SFJAZZ broke ground for a 35,000-square-foot new center for jazz in Hayes Valley, just a few blocks away from the San Francisco Opera House, the San Francisco Symphony, the San Francisco Ballet, the San Francisco Conservatory of Music, Herbst Theatre, and City Hall. Its days as a nomadic music presenter would be coming to an end. In the cultural heart of San Francisco, it was constructing the only free-standing jazz center in the United States, a building that was dedicated to the most American art form.

From an audacious, fledgling urban jazz festival, SFJAZZ had developed into the country's second largest jazz organization—after Jazz at Lincoln Center in New York City—and one of the premier jazz organizations in the world. Forward-looking and determined, it was building its future and creating a permanent space for jazz in San Francisco.

OPPOSITE
**Ukelele virtuoso
Jake Shimabukuro in 2011 at
the Palace of Fine Arts Theatre**

FOLLOWING SPREAD
**Mary Stallings with pianist
Eric Reed in 2012 at Bimbo's
365 Club**

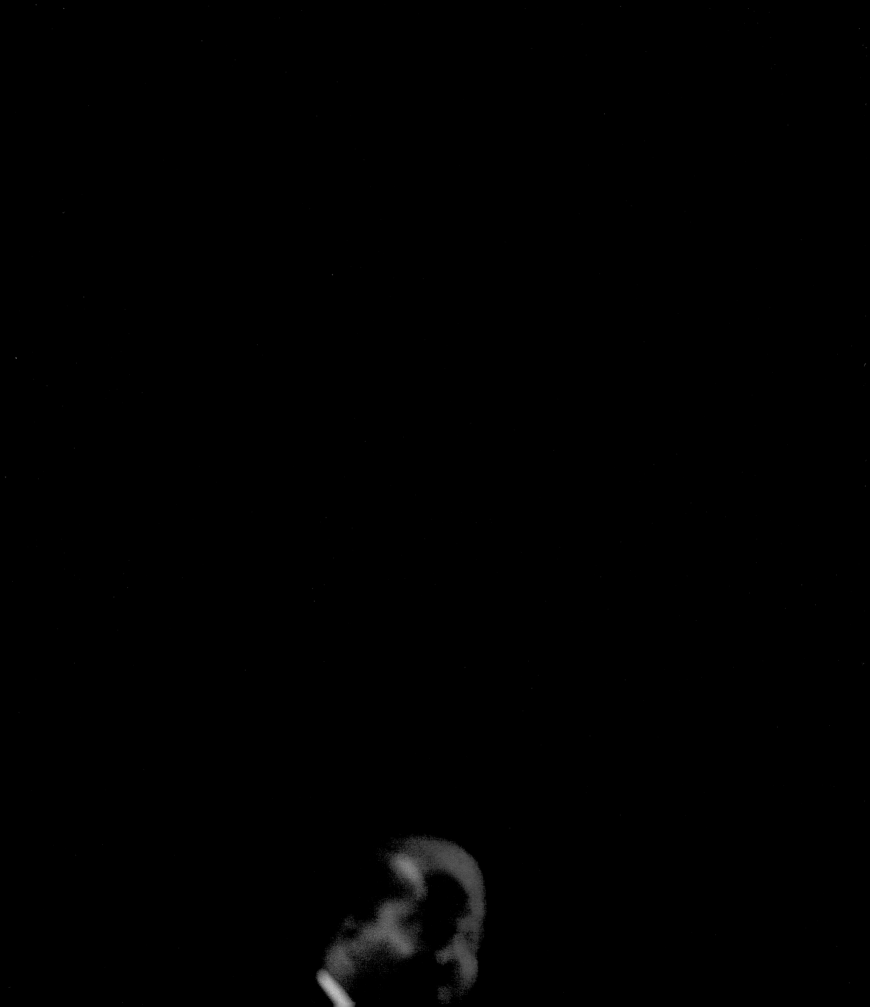

SF JAZZ
CENTER

LOOKING FORWARD

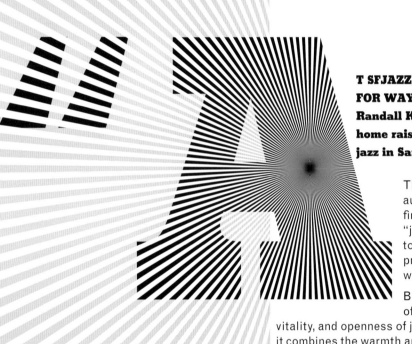

T SFJAZZ, WE AIM HIGH AND LOOK FOR WAYS TO MAKE IT HAPPEN," said Randall Kline. And the organization's new home raises the promise and profile of jazz in San Francisco.

The new building, for jazz artists and audiences, is an affirmation. "For the first time," wrote the *Chicago Tribune*, "jazz in America will have a counterpart to the symphony hall, an edifice that proclaims the value of jazz to anyone who sees it on the street."

But the SFJAZZ Center is not a citadel of culture. Instead, it reflects the energy, vitality, and openness of jazz music. Flexible and transparent, it combines the warmth and intimacy of a small club with the acoustical rigor and quality of a performance hall. "It's a place," Kline said, "where we hope that musicians will love to play and audiences will love to listen."

Designed by award-winning architect Mark Cavagnero and built by Hathaway Dinwiddie Construction Company—with theater consultants Auerbach Pollock Friedlander and SIA Acoustics—the SFJAZZ Center was created from the ground up for the best live jazz experience. "We wanted to make the building vibrant, easily accessible, and intellectually and physically exciting," Cavagnero explained.

The team studied concert halls around the world, through books and the Web, to find the very best elements to incorporate into the new design. The objective was to balance the focus of a formal concert hall with the relaxed, comfortable feel of a club or "found" space like a converted warehouse. Inspiration came from as far away as Muziekcentrum Vredenburg in Utrecht, Netherlands, and the classic Palau Música Catalana in Barcelona, Spain. Kline also put together a list of New York music venues, from casual to formal, where he had heard great performances and where the venue had supported the listening experience. Kline, Cavagnero, theater designer Len Auerbach, acoustician Sam Berkow, and SFJAZZ Executive Operating Director Felice Swapp then traveled to New York and spent two days exploring music venues including Zankel Hall at Carnegie Hall, Jazz at Lincoln Center, the Village Vanguard, Le Poisson Rouge, the Jazz Standard, Anspacher Stage at the Public Theater, and Barbès and the Lyceum in Brooklyn.

ABOVE

**Award-winning architect
Mark Cavagnero designed the
luminous, accessible building
to invite people into the jazz
music experience.**

The SFJAZZ Center's scale, quiet exterior, and sidewalk café integrate it into the surrounding community; the auditorium's steeply raked seating, exceptional acoustics, and flexibility blend the focus of a fomal concert hall and the relaxed, comfortable atmosphere of a club.

High-performance design

The SFJAZZ Center combines the best elements of all these venues in a singular performance space. Its auditorium has steeply raked seating, so that every audience member has a clear view of the stage, and no one is more than forty-five feet away from it. Members of the audience can see each other from every seat because of the "thrust" stage design, which creates a sense of shared experience and communal listening. Performers, in turn, are surrounded, at every angle, by a wall of faces, and the energy they get from the audience fuels the intensity of their performance. "It's a kinetic, comfortable space," Cavagnero said, "and there isn't a bad seat in the house."

The room's top-quality acoustics were specially designed for a wide range of performance types. An acoustical canopy over the stage scatters sound over a wide angle and prevents reflection. The hall's fabric-and-slatted-wood ceiling contains acoustically absorbent elements wherever they're needed for tone and balance. Even the finishes in the auditorium enhance acoustic control. The result, Cavagnero explained, is a room that provides the reverberation, dissipation, and absorption necessary for the audience to hear balance and nuance in the music—whether it's an acoustic guitar, a jazz quartet, or a gospel choir.

Flexibility was a key part of the design. The size of the stage and the capacity of the main hall can be changed as needed for different types of events. The first eight rows of seats can be removed, the stage can be moved toward the seats, and room-reduction banners can descend from the ceiling to change the scale of the room. All the lighting, audio, and other technical systems are flexible and accessible. As a result, the hall can be set up as a three-hundred-fifty-seat, five-hundred-seat, or seven-hundred-seat theater. The room can also be configured for recording sessions, broadcasts, and distance-learning events.

The SFJAZZ Center has practice rooms as well as an eighty-seat multipurpose room for intimate performances, rehearsals, and educational events. The award-winning SFJAZZ High School All-Stars have a permanent new home in the building, as does the SFJAZZ Collective and a new community band for nonprofessional adult musicians. With its new digital learning lab, SFJAZZ can also offer adults and older teens training in digital music literacy. The center creates new educational opportunities, multiplies existing ones, and expands SFJAZZ's connections to the community.

Located in Hayes Valley, at the corner of Franklin and Fell Streets, it's a new cultural gathering place for San Francisco. The SFJAZZ Center is easily accessible by public transportation, car, and bike, and it's part of a dynamic neighborhood. The café will be a convenient place for locals to grab a cup of coffee, a relaxed meal, or a drink. And the building—with a facade that's quiet and restrained during the day but glows and comes alive at night—was carefully planned to integrate into the surrounding community.

FOLLOWING SPREAD

The transparent facade lets passersby see into the SFJAZZ Center's public and rehearsal spaces.

A view of the jazz scene

The building, above all, was designed to invite people into the music. The structure is luminous and transparent. All non-performance and public spaces—including the ground-floor lobby, box office, retail shop, and multipurpose room—have only glass between them and the street. Passersby can watch artists practice and perform, and at Franklin and Fell, they can see into the main hall when the stage is ready for a performance.

"Our goal is to draw people in," Kline said. "We want to make them stop and think, 'I want to see what happens in that building.' For those who are jazz- and culturally inclined, we hope that it will enhance their experiences. For people who think that jazz may be difficult for them to understand, the center is designed to make it easier for them to give it a try and have an appealing experience."

Situated in the center of the city's cultural corridor, the new SFJAZZ Center is a permanent home and gathering place for jazz musicians and lovers of jazz music. Singular, accessible, flexible, and focused on great performance experiences, it reflects the character and aesthetics of SFJAZZ. It also reflects the tremendous support of the members, trustees, individuals, foundations, corporations, government agencies, staff, volunteers, artists, and educators of SFJAZZ. They all made it possible.

The extraordinary SFJAZZ Center is part of SFJAZZ's mission to present the best of the living, breathing, evolving, and expanding tradition of great jazz music in San Francisco. "After thirty years, we're setting the stage for a new beginning," Kline said. "Who knows what's next?"

The SFJAZZ Center moved forward into the future with the input of five talented Resident Artistic Directors. These globally acclaimed jazz musicians and composers—the best in the world at what they do—worked closely with Artistic Director Randall Kline to help shape the center's vision for its first season. Each artist was responsible for two weeks of programming that showcases their own inventive projects and interests. Individually and collaboratively, they imprinted the new SFJAZZ Center's inaugural season with their unique artistic passions and inspiration.

Jason Moran
Piano

MacArthur fellow Jason Moran crosses musical genres, blending jazz, blues, rock, funk, and hip-hop in his compositions and multimedia performances. In 2011 he was named Down Beat's *Jazz Artist of the Year as well as artistic adviser for jazz at the Kennedy Center. He has been on the faculty of the New England Conservatory since 2010.*

"SFJAZZ is way ahead of the curve and wants us to move forward in an adventurous way. One of the pieces I'd like to perform is a suite of music I composed in response to the quilts made by the women of Gee's Bend, Alabama. I took old songs that the women used to sing as they quilted, and I reshaped them.

"I also want to do a dialogue with music and the city's skateboarding community. I live in Harlem, and I remember coming to San Francisco as a kid and bringing my skateboard. Like jazz artists, skaters are always looking at tricks older skaters have done and thinking, 'How can I do that and put a new twist on it?' There's a lot of risk in skating and jazz. In both you're creating and continuing to push forward."

Bill Frisell
Guitar

Widely regarded as the most innovative and influential jazz guitarist to emerge in the 1980s, Grammy-winning artist Bill Frisell has long been exploring the music of America's rural past. A composer and sought-after bandleader, he has launched dozens of unique projects, including The Great Flood, *a suite of original music reflecting on the Mississippi River flood of 1927 and its impact on American society, culture, and music. He has been named* Down Beat *critics' poll Guitarist of the Year nine times.*

"SFJAZZ is very adventurous and has always encouraged me to play my own music. It's been an oasis. That kind of freedom is amazing for me. And the new building is all about the music. When I'm on tour, I'm running from one place to another. But at the SFJAZZ Center, I can have the space and time to let the music develop.

"I want to present musical settings that I wrote for Allen Ginsberg's poem 'Kaddish' and for a Hunter Thompson story. I can't just go into a jazz club and do spoken-word pieces like that.

"I'm also involved in Jason Moran's piece on the Gee's Bend quilts, and there are many people I'd like to do duets with. There are so many opportunities for growing and being stimulated in new ways. It's a chance to take a leap into unknown territory—to take the music further and to learn more."

RESIDENT ARTISTIC DIRECTORS

Miguel Zenón
Alto Saxophone

Multiple Grammy nominee and Guggenheim and MacArthur fellow Miguel Zenón has masterfully balanced and blended the often contradictory poles of innovation and tradition. Widely considered one of the most groundbreaking and influential saxophonists of his generation, he has also developed a unique voice as a composer and a conceptualist, concentrating his efforts on perfecting a fine mix between Latin American folkloric music and jazz. Born and raised in San Juan, Puerto Rico, Zenón has worked with jazz luminaries including Charlie Haden, David Sánchez, The Mingus Big Band, Fred Hersch, Kenny Werner, Bobby Hutcherson, Steve Coleman, and the SFJAZZ Collective. He also topped the Rising Star Alto Sax category of the Down Beat *critics' poll on four occasions.*

"I started working with SFJAZZ as part of the Collective in 2004, the year it started, and I'm part of the SFJAZZ family. I've done performances, listening parties, and educational programs, and I've worked with the High School All-Stars.

"Now, as a Resident Artistic Director, I want to bring the music and artistry of Puerto Rico—and the jazz influenced by it—to a public that isn't familiar with it. Puerto Rican and Latin American music draw from the traditions of the African diaspora, mixed with European and indigenous music. I have been seriously studying the music of Puerto Rico for the last few years.

"One composition that we're planning to perform was born out of a series of interviews I conducted with people of Puerto Rican heritage who were raised around New York City. I wrote modern jazz music around the interviews, and we'll be presenting the piece in a multimedia concert. I'd also like to explore Puerto Rico's popular music of the 1920s and '30s and extend it into the jazz idiom."

John Santos
Percussion

Since the 1970s, no one has done more to maintain and advance the Bay Area's singular synthesis of Caribbean rhythms and postbop forms than percussionist John Santos. A charismatic bandleader, captivating improviser, and dedicated educator, Santos is a master of folkloric traditions from Cuba and Puerto Rico who has consistently found distinctive ways to merge Latin grooves with jazz orchestration. His band Orquesta Batachanga performed at the first Jazz in the City Festival in 1983. Since then he has presented Afro-Cuban music at SFJAZZ, worked as one of its artistic advisers, and led many educational programs. He is a five-time Grammy Award nominee.

"SFJAZZ reflects the Bay Area—it's unique, adventurous, and multicultural, and jazz music doesn't recognize boundaries.

"Miguel Zenón and I are both of Puerto Rican descent, and we want to present the Puerto Rican musical tradition. It's played a big role in jazz on the island and in New York City. Cuban and Puerto Rican music are really two wings of the same bird. They overlap with blues and classical music, Afro-Caribbean rhythms, and music from the Congo and military bands.

"The new SFJAZZ Center brings a lot of official recognition to jazz, but jazz is still connected to the streets. It's important for us to pay attention to ways we can make jazz music economically viable for musicians and keep jazz in the communities where it was born."

Regina Carter
Violin

Improvisational jazz violinist and MacArthur fellow Regina Carter was trained as a classical musician and weaves Motown, bebop, swing, folk, Afro-Caribbean, and world influences into her adventurous vocals and instrumentals. She has performed with Wynton Marsalis, Max Roach, Oliver Lake, Aretha Franklin, Mary J. Blige, Lauryn Hill, Billy Joel, and Dolly Parton.

"European classical orchestras have their halls, built specially for their music. You don't see that so much for America's classical music. In the SFJAZZ Center, we can present jazz the way it should be presented, and the building is a work of art.

"I want to showcase the history of the violin in jazz. Music from all over the planet has some type of instrument related to the violin, and we'll be presenting performances of stringed instruments from Uganda, Senegal, and around the world.

"When I was in college, I played in the saxophone section of a big band. I love big band music, and I'd like to present that too.

"As performing artists, we travel all the time and hear some amazing groups. The SFJAZZ Center is an opportunity for us to bring those experiences to San Francisco and share them with people in a beautiful home and hall. It's an honor to be part of that."

1994: Silent films *Sherlock Junior* and *Go West* starring Buster Keaton with live accompaniment by Bill Frisell Band; Dave Brubeck Quartet, Gerry Mulligan Quartet; Tuck and Patti, Claudia Gomez; Jim Cullum Jazz Band with Nicolas Payton; Abbey Lincoln, Betty Carter (with Geri Allen, Jack DeJohnette, Dave Holland); Don Pullen's African Brazilian Connection, Bheki Mseleku; Larry Vuckovich International All-Stars; Berkeley High School Ensemble; Wayne Horvitz/Robin Holcombe and New York Jazz Composers West, Jai Utal's Pagan Love Orchestra; Madeline Eastman, Kitty Margolis; Manny Oquendo's Libre with Andy Gonzalez; "Jazz at the Philharmonic, 50th Anniversary" with Illinois Jacquet Big Band, J.J. Johnson Quintet, Tommy Flanagan, Al McKibbon, Roy Haynes; Terra Sul, Claudia Villela, Wild Mango; Al Plank and Noel Jewkes; Jerry Granelli (with Jane Ira Bloom, Anthony Cox, and Jullian Priester); Charlie Haden's Quartet West; "11th Street Block Party" with James T. Kirk, Alphabet Soup, Charlie Hunter Trio, Mingus Amungus, Dog Slyde, Jazz on the Line; premiere of *Tone Dialing* with Ornette Coleman's PrimeTime, Ornette Coleman New Quartet (with Geri Allen, Charnette Moffett, Denardo Coleman); Branford Marsalis Quartet, Sonny Simmons Trio; Keith Jarrett, solo

1995: Modern Jazz Quartet; Keith Jarrett, Jack DeJohnette, Gary Peacock; "11th Street Block Party" with Jimmy Smith and Damn! (with Mark Whitfield, Nicholas Payton, Christian McBride), Broun Fellinis, Dogslyde, John Tchicai and the Archetypes; Splatter Trio with Myra Melford; Gunn High School Big Band and Combo; Joe Lovano Trio, Jacky Terrasson Trio, Charlie Hunter Trio; "Randy Weston Salute" with Randy Weston, African Rhythms Trio, Volcano Blues Band conducted by Melba Liston (with Robert Jr. Lockwood, Teddy Edwards, Bennie Powell, Charlie Persip); "Tribute to Armando Peraza" with Armando Peraza, Al McKibbon, Emil Richards, Francisco Aguabella, Orestes Vilató, John Santos's Machete Ensemble; "Bessie Smith Tribute" with Pat Yankee, Lavay Smith, Denise Perrier; "Charlie Parker 75th Anniversary" with Slide Hampton and the Jazzmasters Orchestra (with Phil Woods, Jimmy Heath, Charles McPherson, James Moody); Toninho Horta, Wild Mango, Brasilian Beat with the Escola Nova De Samba Dancers; Noel Jewkes's Dr. Legato Special; "Acid Jazz" with Slide Five, New Legends, Kelly Huff, Better Daze, DJ Grey Boy; Ed Kelly Trio, Terrence Kelly with the Oakland Interfaith Choir, Pete Escovedo and Shelia E.; Cecil Taylor Orchestra; Ralph Kirshbaum plays Bach Solo Cello Suites; Wayne Shorter Sextet, Christian McBride Quartet; "California Blues: A Tribute to Swingtime Records" with Johnny Otis, Charles Brown, Jay McShann, Lowell Fulson, Jimmy Witherspoon, Jimmy McCracklin, Earl Brown; "The Music of Antonio Carlos Jobim" with Joe Henderson and Herbie Hancock

1996: Sonny Rollins; San Francisco Bay Area Grammy All-Star High School Jazz Band; George Shearing Quintet, Diana Krall Trio; "Silk Road: Asian Concepts in Jazz" with Zakir Hussain, Mark Izu, Miya Masaoka, Frances Wong, Hafez Modirzadeh, Anthony Brown; Jazz Passengers with Deborah Harry, Peter Apfelbaum Sextet; "Stride Piano Summit" with Dr. Billy Taylor, Al Casey, Doc Cheatham, Jay McShann, Dick Hyman, Ralph Sutton, Mike Lipskin; David Sanborn Group, Charlie Hunter and Scott Amendola; "Sacred Space: A Tribute to Don Cherry" with Charlie Haden, Dewey Redman, Naná Vasconcelos, Peter Apfelbaum; Dick Hyman; Dee Dee Bridgewater with Jacky Terrasson, Mark Murphy; Mingus Amungus, Grassy Knoll; Robert Stewart, Josh Jones Quartet, Dogslyde; Dave Ellis Quartet, Papa's Culture, Ann Dyer and No Good Time Fairies, Oranj Symphonette, Will Bernard Quartet, DJ Andrew; Max Roach, Leon Parker Quartet; Michael Ray and the Cosmic Krewe, Leroy Jones Quintet, Bo Grumpus, DJ Cheb I Sabbah and 1002 Nights; John Lee Hooker, Ruth Brown, Charlie Musselwhite; Chico O'Farrill Orchestra, Candi Sosa; "Three Guitars" with Paco de Lucía, Al Di Meola, John McLaughlin; Mary Stallings, Paula West; B-3 Summit with Jack McDuff, Shirley Scott, Duke Jethro; *Midnight in the Garden of Good and Evil* with John Berendt (author), Emma Kelly, Lady Chablis, Margaret Whiting, Julius LaRosa, Warren Vache, John Pizzarelli, Bill Charlap; "Percussion Maestros of North and South India" with Ustad Alla Rakha, Zakir Hussain, Pharoah Sanders

1997: Nancy Wilson, Joe Williams; Northern California Grammy All-Star High School Big Band; Don Byron "Bug Music" Septet, Graham Connah Group; Sonny Rollins; Gato Barbieri, Braxton Brothers; Cassandra Wilson, Charlie Hunter Group; Danilo Perez Trio, Dmitri Matheny and Bill Douglass; Celia Cruz with Jose Alberto "El Canario" Orquesta, Albita; Toshiko Akiyoshi Jazz Orchestra with Lew Tabackin

and Miya Masaoka; Dick Hyman, William Carter, John Gill, Rex Allen, Bob Schulz, Clint Baker; Elvin Jones Jazz Machine, Roy Haynes Group, Charles Lloyd/ Billy Higgins; Gonzalo Rubalcaba Trio, Omar Sosa and John Santos; Lavay Smith and Her Red Hot Skillet Lickers, David Hardiman's S.F. All-Star Big Band; "Tribute to Orrin Keepnews" with Jimmy Heath, Gary Bartz, Tootie Heath, Mulgrew Miller, Nat Adderley, Randy Weston, Bob Cranshaw; "Rova 20th" with Rova Saxophone Quartet, What We Live, Glenn Spearman Double Trio, Actual Size, John Raskin Quintet, Adams and Connah Group; Joshua Redman, Christian McBride, Brian Blade; Jimmy McGriff, Booker T. Jones, Hank Crawford; "Nicholas Brothers Tribute" with Nicholas Brothers, Count Basie Orchestra, Bunny Briggs, Donald O'Connor, Williams Brothers, "Porgy and Bess" with Joe Henderson, Tommy Flanagan, Rickie Lee Jones, Dave Holland, Conrad Herwig, Stefon Harris, Jason Marsalis; Jean-Yves Thibaudet; Mike Marshall and Choro Famoso, Adriana Moreno and Carlos Oliveira; George Winston; "Charles Brown 75th Birthday" with Charles Brown Quintet and Big Band, Bonnie Raitt, John Lee Hooker, Ruth Brown, Jimmy Scott; "Blood on the Fields," Wynton Marsalis and the Lincoln Center Jazz Orchestra with Jon Hendricks, Cassandra Wilson; Chick Corea "Remembering Bud Powell" Band (with Roy Haynes, Wallace Roney, Kenny Garrett, and Christian McBride), McCoy Tyner

1998: Etta James, The Dirty Dozen; Medeski Martin and Wood, Bill Frisell (with Jim Keltner and Viktor Krauss); Al Jarreau; Gunn High School Jazz Ensemble; "Legacy of Charlie Mingus" with Mingus Big Band, Charles McPherson Quartet with Jimmy Knepper, Mingus Amungus; Ivan Lins, Claudia Villela and Ricardo Peixoto; Poncho Sanchez; Fred Hersch; Diana Krall, David Frishberg; Lavay Smith and Her Red Hot Skillet Lickers, Hot Club of San Francisco; "Benny Goodman Tribute" with Dick Hyman, Kenny Daven, Warren Vache, Dan Barrett, Howard Alden; "Sacred Space" with Yusef Lateef and Adam Rudolph, Charlie Haden and Tom Harrell, Ann Dyer Trio; Joshua Redman Quartet, Andy Narell Group; Ruben Gonzalez with Ibrahim Ferrer, Chucho Valdés Quartet; Broun Fellinis, Tin Hat Trio, Dmitri Matheny Trio, Pothole, Steve Lucky and the Rhumba Bums; Bobby Watson's Art Blakey Project (with James Williams, Brian Lynch, Billy Pierce, Ralph Peterson, and Essiet Okon Essiet), Mel Martin's Bebop and Beyond 2000; Sphere (Kenny Barron, Gary Bartz, Buster Williams, Ben Riley), Geri Allen, Ellis Marsalis; "B-3 Summit" with Charles Earland, Big John Patton, Ed Kelly Quartet with Robert Stewart; Rosemary Clooney, Kevin Mahogany; "Violin Summit" with Joe Kennedy, Regina Carter, Johnny Frigo, Darol Anger, Matt Glaser; Andy Bey; Fred Ho's Monkey Orchestra, Zakir Hussain; Andy Statman Quartet, Kaila Flexer and Third Ear; "Fiesta Boricua" with Marc Anthony, El Gran Combo, John Santos and the Machete Ensemble; Corey Harris, Lady Bianca; David Sanchez Sextet and Chamber Orchestra, Rebeca Mauleón Quartet with Orestes Vilató; John Zorn's Masada, John Schott Group; "Good Vibes" Milton Jackson with Cedar Walton Quartet, Bobby Hutcherson Quartet, Stefon Harris Quartet

1999: Keith Jarrett, Gary Peacock, Jack DeJohnette; Sonny Rollins; Cassandra Wilson; Charlie Haden's Quartet West with Strings, Shirley Horn Trio; Berkeley High School Jazz Ensemble; Chick Corea and Origin with Gary Burton, Gonzalo Rubalcaba Trio; Henry Kaiser and Wadada Leo Smith's "Yo Miles!", The New Art Jazz Quartet (James "Blood" Ulmer, Rashied Ali, Reggie Workman, John Hicks); Gerald Wilson Orchestra, Louie Bellson Big Band plus Queen Esther Marrow and Jon Faddis; Gato Barbieri; Tito Puente, Eddie Palmieri, Israel "Cachao" Lopez; David Murray's Fo Deuk Revue, E.W. Wainwright's African Roots of Jazz; Kenny Wheeler/Kenny Werner; Indigo Swing, Jim Cullum Jazz Band, Lavay Smith and Her Red Hot Skillet Lickers; "Sacred Space" with Jackie McClean, Steve Lacy; Jesus Diaz QBA, Los Mocosos, Mazacote, Orquesta La Moderna Tradicion, Josh Jones Latin Ensemble; Paolo Conte; Dave Douglas Tiny Bell Trio, Tin Hat Trio; Tommy Flanagan Trio, Benny Green; "B-3 Summit" with Jimmy Smith, Joey DeFrancesco; Philip Glass and Kronos Quartet accompanying the 1931 film *Dracula*; Patricia Barber Trio; Etta James, Joe Louis Walker and Boss Talkers; Virginia Rodrigues; Richard Bona Group; Vivendo De Pao, Adriana Moreno and Ciganos; The Klezmatics, San Francisco Klezmer Experience; Brad Mehldau; Paco de Lucía; "Buena Vista Social Club" with Orquesta Ibrahim Ferrer, Rubén González y Su Grupo, Company Segundo

Spring 2000: Joshua Redman, solo; "Music of Wayne Shorter" with Wayne Shorter Group, Joe Lovano, Branford Marsalis, Joshua Redman, Brad Mehldau Trio with

Robert Hurst and Gregory Hutchinson; Joe Lovano Group; Pat Metheny Trio; "A Salute to Jim Hall" with Jim Hall Trio, Bill Frisell, Rusell Malone, Peter Bernstein, John Abercrombie, Pat Metheny, Greg Osby, Bill Charlap, Tom Harrell, Chris Potter; "Fusion on Film" hosted by Steve Smith; Joe Zawinul Syndicate, Richard Bona Group; "History of Jazz Drumming on Film" hosted by Elvin Jones; Elvin Jones Jazz Machine, Brian Blade Fellowship; Barbarito Torres; Arturo Sandoval Group, David Sanchez Group; John Santos and Machete Ensemble (with Orestes Vilató, Jose Antonio Fajardo, Felo Barrio, Nelson Gonzalez)

SFJF 2000: Cesária Évora; Omara Portuondo; Abbey Lincoln, Jimmy Scott with Hank Crawford; Berkeley High School Jazz Ensemble; The Jazz Mandolin Project, Will Bernard Group; Lee Konitz and Paul Bley, Trio 3 (Oliver Lake, Reggie Workman, Andrew Cyrille); Lou Rawls, Ruth Brown; Celia Cruz, Oscar D'Leon; Cecil Taylor; Jane Bunnett and the Spirits of Havana; Paula West; Russell Malone Quartet, Julian Lage/Randy Vincent; "Sacred Space" with Joe Lovano, Greg Osby; Russell Gunn's Ethnomusicology, Trevor Watts Moire Music Group; Andrew Hill Sextet, Jason Moran Trio; "B-3 Summit" with Barbara Dennerlein, Rhoda Scott, Trudy Pitts; "SFJAZZ Beacon Award" with Eddie Marshall, Holy Mischief, Bobby McFerrin, Bobby Hutcherson, Freddie Hubbard, Fourth Way Reunion (Eddie Marshall, Mike Nock, Michael White); Bud Shank Sextet, Noel Jewkes Legato Express; Eliades Ochoa, Orquesta Aragon, Cubanismo; McCoy Tyner, solo; Robert Cray, Duke Robillard Group with Herb Ellis, Eric Bibb; Lavay Smith and Her Red Hot Skillet Lickers, The Blue Room Boys; Toots Thielemans with Oscar Castro-Neves and Kenny Werner; Marcio Faraco; Keith Jarrett, Gary Peacock, Jack DeJohnette; "Remember Shakti" with John McLaughlin, Zakir Hussain, U. Srininvas

Spring 2001: Nicholas Payton's Louis Armstrong Centennial Celebration, Randy Sandke's Armstrong All-Stars with Kenny Davern and Wycliffe Gordon; "The Music of Freddie Hubbard and Woody Shaw" with Terence Blanchard, Kenny Garrett, Bobby Hutcherson, Steve Turre, Cedar Walton, Eddie Henderson, Brian Lynch, Ingrid Jensen; Andy Bey Trio, Patricia Barber; Paolo Conte; Brenda Boykin and the Eric Swinderman Quartet; Dianne Reeves, Jane Monheit; "Black, White, and Beyond" panel with Dr. Harry Edwards, Steve Coleman, Dr. Angela Davis, Nat Hentoff, Bruce Lundvall, Richard M. Sudhalter; Avishai Cohen Quintet, Matt Small's Crushing Spiral Ensemble; Joshua Redman Quartet, Russell Gunn's Ethnomusicology; Geri Allen; Marcus Roberts; Gonzalo Rubalcaba; Ray Brown Trio, Christian McBride Band; Dave Holland Quintet, Mingus Amungus; Joshua Redman/Christian McBride

SFJF 2001: Max Roach Quartet (with Cecil Bridgewater, Tyrone Brown, Odean Pope); "John Coltrane 75th Anniversary" with McCoy Tyner, Tommy Flanagan Trio, Pharoah Sanders Quartet; Kenny Barron/Regina Carter, Harvey Wainapel/John Wiitala; Odean Pope Quartet with David Murray; Etta James, Joe Louis Walker; Rosemary Clooney, Paula West; Don Byron's Music for Six Musicians; Zydeco Flames, Aux Cajunals; Terry Riley/Krishna Bhatt; Fred Frith/Miya Masaoka/Larry Ochs Trio; Bobby Short and His Orchestra; Bill Frisell with Greg Leisz and Vinicius Cantuária; "SFJAZZ Beacon Award" with Vernon Alley, Allen Smith, Noel Jewkes; Charlie Haden's Nocturne with Gonzalo Rubalcaba and Joe Lovano; "B-3 Summit" with Reuben Wilson, Leon Spencer; Mary Stallings with Eric Reed Quartet; The Brad Mehldau Trio; "Sacred Space" with Charles Lloyd and Zakir Hussain; Manolín; The Dave Brubeck Quartet; Joanne Brackeen; "The Music of Rahsaan Roland Kirk" with James Carter, Steve Turre, Mulgrew Miller, Vincent Herring, Buster Williams, Lewis Nash; Denny Zeitlin Trio with Buster Williams and Matt Wilson; Dick Hyman, Ed Polcer, Kenny Davern, Howard Alden; Keith Jarrett, Gary Peacock, Jack DeJohnette

Spring 2002: "Women and Jazz" panel with Angela Davis, Maria Schneider, Sherrie Tucker, Mary Watkins, Susie Ibarra; Marilyn Crispell Trio with Gary Peacock and Paul Motian, Susie Ibarra Quartet; Maria Schneider Orchestra with Ingrid Jensen; Cassandra Wilson; Jane Ira Bloom Quartet, Jane Bunnett and Spirits of Havana; Stanton Moore (with Chris Wood, Skerik, Brian Seeger, John Ellis), Scott Amendola Group; "B-3 Summit" with Dr. Lonnie Smith Trio (with James Carter and Lenny White), Larry Goldings Trio; Omara Portuondo; "The Bridge, Revisited" Joshua Redman, Bill Frisell, Brian Blade, Larry Grenadier; David S. Ware Quartet; Sonny Rollins; Joe Lovano, David Sanchez, Lew Tabackin, Robert Stewart, Benny Green Trio; Omar Sosa Septet, Anthony Brown's Asian American Orchestra; Enrico Rava Quintet,

Richard Galliano; Esbjörn Svensson Trio (EST), Bugge Wesseltoft; Wynton Marsalis Septet; Herbie Hancock, Michael Brecker, Roy Hargrove

SFJF 2002: SFJAZZ All-Star High School Ensemble; Dirty Dozen Brass Band, Rebirth Brass Band, Nicholas Payton and the Soul Patrol, Zigaboo Modeliste and the Aahkesstra, Donald Harrison and Idris Muhammad's Congo Nation Indians, Mitch Woods's Big Easy Boogie; Jon Jang's "Up from the Root" (with David Murray and Melody of China), Vijay Iyer /Rudresh Mahanthappa; Charlie Hunter/Idris Muhammad, Djelimady Tounkara, Caetano Veloso; Rubén Blades, Eric Rigler and Boca Livre; James "Blood" Ulmer, Yohimbe Brothers with Vernon Reid, DJ Logic, Johnny A; Wayne Shorter Quartet, Branford Marsalis Quartet; "Benny Goodman Tribute" Eddie Daniels (with Bucky Pizzarelli and Joe Locke), Jim Rothermel's Neo Classic Swing; Jane Monheit, Bill Charlap Trio; Elvin Jones Jazz Machine, McCoy Tyner Big Band; Hermeto Pascoal, Banda Mantiqueira; "SFJAZZ Beacon Award" with Ed Kelly with Robert Stewart, Michele Rosewoman, Eddie Marshall, David Hardiman, Khalil Shaheed, Babatunde Lea, Ron Belcher, Jules Broussard, Oakland Interfaith Gospel Choir; Michel Camilo Trio; Jack DeJohnette/John Surman, Paul Plimley/Lisle Ellis; Tin Hat Trio and Orchestra, Japonize Elephants; Yusef Lateef and Adam Rudolph, "Sacred Space" with James Carter, Huun-Huur-Tu; Lynne Arriale Trio; Greg Osby Quartet with Eric Reed, Herbie Nichols Project; Shirley Horn Trio, Ahmad Jamal Trio; Toshiko Akiyoshi; Ellis Marsalis/Bobby Hutcherson, Bruce Forman/John Wiitala; Toots Thielemans with Oscar Castro-Neves and Kenny Werner; Patricia Barber, Graham Connah Group; Ornette Coleman; "Bob Wills Tribute" with Merle Haggard, Lost Weekend; Vicente Amigo; Bobby McFerrin and mystery guests; Charles Lloyd (with Geri Allen, John Abercrombie, Robert Hurst, Adam Nussbaum), Tomasz Stanko; Lavay Smith and Her Red Hot Skillet Lickers, Quintet of the Hot Club of San Francisco; Mark Murphy, Kurt Elling

Spring 2003: Marcus Roberts Trio; Eddie Palmieri and La Perfecta II, India, Spanish Harlem Orchestra; Herbie Hancock Quartet; Ibrahim Ferrer; Quincy Troupe, Oliver Lake Steel Quartet; Edgar Meyer/Mike Marshall; Kenny Burrell Quartet, Benny Green/ Russell Malone; Sekou Sundiata Band, Daughters of Yam; Charlie Haden's American Dreams with Michael Brecker; Ken Nordine; Chucho Valdés Quartet with Joe Lovano, Gonzalo Rubalcaba Trio; Randy Weston's African Rhythms Duo with John Handy, Ray Bryant; Campbell Brothers; Joshua Redman's Elastic Band; Kenny Baron Trio; Jason Moran and the Bandwagon, The Bad Plus; Mark O'Connor's Hot Swing Trio, Johnny Frigo; Martial Solal Trio, Moutin Reunion Quartet; Charlie Haden/Jim Hall; Charlie Haden, Dewey Redman, Joshua Redman; Dave Brubeck Quartet; João Gilberto

SFJF 2003: McCoy Tyner; SFJAZZ All-Star High School Ensemble; Peter Cincotti, Julian Lage Trio; Mavis Staples; Terry Riley's "Sun Rings" with Kronos Quartet; Gabriele Mirabassi/Luciano Biondini, Gianluigi Trovesi/Gianni Coscia; Omara Portuondo, Virgínia Rodrigues; Ann Hampton Callaway and the Larry Dunlap Trio with the SFJAZZ All-Star High School Big Band; Dave Holland Quintet; Ruth Brown, Joe Louis Walker; Cecil Taylor; Enrico Rava Quartet with Paolo Fresu, Doctor 3; Enrico Rava/Stefano Bollani Duo, Danilo Rea; Etta James; René Marie; Maria Muldaur, Dan Hicks; "SFJAZZ Beacon Award," Phil Elwood with Mel Martin, Kim Nalley, Leon Oakley's Friends of Jazz, Denise Perrier, Larry Vuckovich, Denny Zeitlin; Chano Domínguez with Jerry Gonzalez; "B-3 Summit" with Jimmy Smith, Joey DeFrancesco; Bill Frisell and the Intercontinentals, Marc Ribot y Los Cubanos Postizos; Marian McPartland; Nancy Wilson, Ramsey Lewis; Lavay Smith and Her Red Hot Skillet Lickers, Swing Fever with Denise Perrier; Kitty Margolis; Keith Jarrett, Jack DeJohnette, Gary Peacock

Spring 2004: Preservation Hall Jazz Band; Savion Glover and Ti Dii; Ornette Coleman; SFJAZZ Collective; Charles Lloyd; Sam Rivers (with Reggie Workman, Jason Moran), William Parker Quartet; Paul Bley, Satoko Fujii; Toots Thielemans (with Airto, Oscar Castro-Neves, Kenny Werner); Wayne Shorter Quartet, Brad Mehldau Trio; Joe Zawinul Syndicate; Joshua Redman; Orchestra Baobab; "Tribute to Charlie Parker" with Gary Bartz, Sonny Fortune, Vincent Herring with Ronnie Matthews/Cecil McBee/ Billy Hart, Bebop and Beyond; Poncho Sanchez, Rebeca Mauleón Quartet; Jimmy Scott, Madeline Eastman; "Music of Stan Getz" with Bill Charlap Trio, Trio Da Paz, Harry Allen, Harvey Wainapel; Chris Potter Quartet, Fly (Mark Turner, Larry Grenadier, Jeff Ballard); Hank Jones Trio with Clark Terry; Béla Fleck/Edgar Meyer; Darol Anger/

Philip Aaberg; Tomasz Stanko Quartet; Matthew Shipp; David Sánchez Quartet and Strings perform Stan Getz's "Focus"; Hugh Masekela; Sonny Rollins; João Gilberto

SFJF 2004: SFJAZZ All-Star High School Big band; "Sacred Space" with Charlie Haden, Jane Ira Bloom; Caetano Veloso; Don Byron's Ivey-Divey Trio with Jason Moran and Jack DeJohnette; Vijay Iyer and Mike Ladd; Plays Monk: Scott Amendola/Ben Goldberg/Devin Hoff; Yosuke Yamashite; Mariza; Brad Mehldau; Al Di Meola/Stanley Clarke/Jean-Luc Ponty; Mary Stallings; Rokia Traoré; Lavay Smith and Her Red Hot Skillet Lickers, Le Jazz Hot Quartet; Ojos De Brujo; Kurt Elling, Stacey Kent, "SFJAZZ Beacon Award" with Allen Smith with Larry Vuckovich, Jeff Chambers, Omar Clay; Sex Mob; Monksieland Band (with Roswell Rudd, Dave Douglas, Marty Ehrlich), Jessica Williams; Mark O'Connor's Hot Swing Trio; Michel Camilo Trio, and solo; "B-3 Summit" with Jimmy McGriff Quartet, Masters of Groove (with Reuben Wilson, Grant Green Jr., Bernard Purdue); film The Creature from the Black Lagoon with live accompaniment by the Jazz Passsengers; Dena DeRose; Dmitri Matheny Group; Dianne Reeves; Hermeto Pascoal Band; Eddie Marshall's Holy Mischief Ensemble; Jim Hall Trio, Kurt Rosenwinkel Group; Jaga Jazzist, Supersilent; Gonzalo Rubalcaba Trio; Etta James, Earl Thomas; Gary Burton Quartet with Julian Lage and Makoto Ozone; The Conga Kings (with Candido, "Patato" Valdez, Giovanni Hidalgo), Plena Libre; "Tribute to Fats Waller" with Ruth Brown, Dick Hyman, Jay McShann, Marty Grosz, Mike Lipskin

Spring 2005: SFJAZZ Collective; Branford Marsalis Quartet, Ravi Coltrane Group; "Roy Haynes 80th Birthday" with Roy Haynes, Chick Corea, Gary Burton, Kenny Garrett, Nicholas Payton, Joshua Redman, Christian McBride; Solomon Burke; Larry Coryell, Badi Assad, John Abercrombie; Ahmad Jamal; Orchestra Baobab; Avishai Cohen Group, Anthony Coleman's Sephardic Tinge; "Coltrane's Asecension 40th Anniversary" Orkestrova with Rova Saxophone Quartet (with Nels Cline, Fred Frith, Carla Kihlstedt, Ikue Mori, Otomo Yoshihide); Lou Donaldson with Dr. Lonnie Smith and David "Fathead" Newman; Preservation Hall Jazz Band; Dave Brubeck Quartet; Maria Rita; Matt Wilson's Arts and Crafts Band; Mingus Big Band; Shirley Horn; Tord Gustavsen Trio; Dee Dee Bridgewater; Ivan Lins; John Santos's Machete Ensemble; SFJAZZ All-Star High School Ensemble with Terence Blanchard; Terence Blanchard Sextet; Ravi Shankar with Anoushka Shankar; Sonny Rollins; Jason Moran and the Bandwagon; Madeleine Peyroux; Manhattan Transfer; "Music of Rahsaan Roland Kirk" (with Steve Turre, James Carter, Vincent Herring, Mulgrew Miller, Buster Williams, Winard Harper); Realistic Orchestra, Jesus Diaz y QBA, Transmission Trio, DJ Aspect; "Coltrane's Crescent" (with McCoy Tyner, Joshua Redman, Brian Blade, Reginald Veal); Rashied Ali/Sonny Fortune; The Bad Plus, Christopher O'Riley; Frank Morgan/Cyrus Chestnut; Joshua Redman, Dave Liebman, Joe Lovano; Michael Wolff/Badal Roy; Joshua Redman's Elastic Band, Nicholas Payton's Sonic Trance; Paula West with Eric Reed Trio, Andy Bey

SFJF 2005: SFJAZZ All-Star High School Big Band with Youth Speaks Poets; Abbey Lincoln; World Saxophone Quartet (David Murray, Oliver Lake, Hamiet Bluiett, Bruce Williams); Omar Sosa Quartet, Dafnis Prieto Quintet; Lalah Hathaway, Marcus Miller; Eldar; Etta James; Tierney Sutton Band; Dave Douglas and Keystone; "SFJAZZ Beacon Award Concert": Bill Bell with Dave Ellis, Charles McNeal, Eddie Marshall, Jeff Chambers, Dmitiri Matheny; Mose Allison, Patricia Barber; George Gables Project (with Gary Bartz, Jeff "Tain" Watts, Eric Revis, and Bobby Hutcherson); John Scofield; Keren Ann; Yusef Lateef (with Adam Rudolph, Joseph Bowie, Sylvie Courvoisier); Poncho Sanchez Latin Jazz Band; Paris Combo, Le Jazz Hot; "Klezmer Clarinet" Don Byron; Bill Charlap Trio, Denny Zeitlin Trio; Gangbé Brass Band; Inti-Ilimani; Eva Ayllon; Barbara Cook; Bobo Stenson; Virgínia Rodrigues; Ornette Coleman Quartet; Jacqui Naylor; Toots Thielemans (with Kenny Werner, Oscar Castro-Neves, Airto); Konono N° 1, Dan Zanes and Friends; Blind Boys of Alabama, Fairfield Four

Spring 2006: Le Mystère des Voix Bulgares; Eartha Kitt; Keith Jarrett, solo; Chris Botti, David Sanborn; Ellis Marsalis Quartet; ICP Orchestra; Irvin Mayfield and the New Orleans Jazz Orchestra; Henry Threadgill's Zooid; Enrico Rava/Stefano Bollani, Enrico Pieranunzi; John Pizzarelli, Taylor Eigsti/Julian Lage; Robert Glasper Trio; SFJAZZ Collective; Pharoah Sanders; Randy Weston's African Rhythms and The Gnawa Master Musicians of Morocco; Maria Rita; Dewey Redman Quartet; João

Bosco; Kenny Barron Trio, Danilo Pérez Trio; Phil Woods Quintet; Gonzalo Rubalcaba; Ray Barretto; Jimmy Scott; SFJAZZ High School All-Stars with Joshua Redman; Savion Glover; Shelly Berg Trio; Paquito D'Rivera Quintet; Baaba Maal; Kenny Werner and Claudia Villela

SFJF 2006: Planet Drum with Mickey Hart, Zakir Hussain, Sikiru Adepoju, Giovanni Hidalgo; SFJAZZ All-Star High School Ensemble; Sonny Rollins; Badi Assad; James Cotton Blues Band with Hubert Sumlin; Lavay Smith and Her Red Hot Skillet Lickers, Steve Lucky and the Rhumba Bums; Meshell Ndegeocello; "Jimmy Heath's 80th Birthday Celebration" with the Heath Brothers with Jeremy Pelt; Stefon Harris and Blackout!, Miguel Zenón Quartet; Cyrus Chestnut and Russell Malone Quartet, Lionel Loueke Trio; Toshiko Akiyoshi; Arturo Sandoval; Pablo Ziegler Trio for Nuevo Tango; Andrew Hill Quintet, Nels Cline Group; Kamikaze Ground Crew; Joe Zawinul Syndicate; "B-3 Summit" with Dr. Lonnie Smith, James Carter Organ Trio; Charles Lloyd's Sangam with Zakir Hussain and Eric Harland; Myra Melford; Alice Coltrane (with Ravi Coltrane, Charlie Haden, and Roy Haynes); Marisa Monte; Django Reinhardt Festival with Dorado Schmitt; Montclair Women's Big Band with Linda Tillery and Allison Miller; "SFJAZZ Beacon Award Concert": Mary Stallings with Marcus Shelby Big Band with Geri Allen; Mimi Fox Trio; Ahmad Jamal; Roswell Rudd and The Mongolian Buryat Band; Ana Moura; John Santos and the Machete Ensemble (with Jerry Medina, Ray Vega, Maria Marquez)

Spring 2007: Ladysmith Black Mambazo; Fred Hersch; Jerry Gonzalez and the Fort Apache Band; Omar Sosa; Etta James, Joe Louis Walker; SFJAZZ Collective; "Sacred Space" with Bill Frisell; Poncho Sanchez; Dave Holland Quintet; Dianne Reeves; Anoushka Shankar; Ben Riley's Monk Legacy Band, Geri Allen Trio; Freddie Cole with Houston Person, Madeline Eastman; Dave Brubeck Quartet and Big Band; Dulce Pontes; Assad Brothers with Turtle Island String Quartet; Dino Saluzzi and Anja Lechner; "Monk/Coltrane Carnegie Hall" (with Joshua Redman, Brad Mehldau, Christian McBride, Brian Blade); Gabriela Montero; "B-3 Summit" with Joey De Francesco Trio with George Coleman, Trudy Pitts Trio; McCoy Tyner; Allen Toussaint, Henry Butler; Angelique Kidjo; Eddie Palmieri /David Sanchez; "Monk Town Hall Concert" with Jason Moran with T.S. Monk; Guillermo Klein y Los Guachos; Joshua Redman Trio Plays Monk (with Scott Amendola, Ben Goldberg, and Devin Hoff); Cesária Évora; Sasha Dobson; SFJAZZ All-Star High School Ensemble with Stefon Harris; Paula West; "Stride Piano Summit" with Dick Hyman, Butch Thompson, Mike Lipskin; Carlinhos Brown, Ojos De Brujo

SFJF 2007: John McLaughlin, Kevin Eubanks; Pharoah Sanders; Toots Thielemans; Dee Dee Bridgewater; Marcus Shelby Orchestra, Jon Jang Seven; Issac Delgado; Ahmad Jamal; Sara Tavares; T.S. Monk Sextet, Monk's Music Trio; Kronos Quartet, Glenn Kotche; Preservation Hall Jazz Band; Dr. John; Anat Cohen; Pete Escovedo; Big Chief Bo Dollis and The Wild Magnolias; Jacky Terrasson; Ornette Coleman; Willem Breuker Kollektief; Fred Hersch Trio plus Ralph Alessi and Chris Cheek; Ravi Shankar; Jason Moran commission "In My Mind"; Céu; John Abercrombie Quartet; Jacqui Naylor, Spencer Day; Tinariwen; Tord Gustavsen; Paquito D'Rivera; Dorado Schmitt's Django Reinhardt Festival; Vieux Farka Touré; Kneebody, Happy Apple; Joe Lovano Quintet, Renee Rosnes Quartet; The Conga Kings (with Giovanni Hidalgo, Patato Valdez, and Candido); Kurt Elling, Nancy King; Herbie Hancock, Gonzalo Rubalcaba; Cristina Branco; SFJAZZ All-Star High School Ensemble; Caetano Veloso; Youssou N'Dour; Chava Alberstein; Le Mystère des Voix Bulgares

Spring 2008: Toumani Diabaté's Symmetric Orchestra; Oscar Castro-Neves; Travis Sullivan's Bjorkestra, Realistic Orchestra; Nik Bärtsch's Ronin, The Frequency; Two Foot Yard, Iron and Albatross; Keith Jarrett, Gary Peacock and Jack DeJohnette; Third World Love, Yaron Herman Trio; McCoy Tyner and Savion Glover; Regina Carter Quintet; Denny Zeitlin; Charles Lloyd New Quartet (with Jason Moran, Reuben Rogers, Eric Harland); Hiromi; "The Latin Side of Wayne Shorter" with Conrad Herwig and Eddie Palmieri; Joe Sample; Wayne Shorter Quartet with Imani Winds; silent films Sherlock Jr., The Cabinet of Dr. Caligari, Nosferatu accompanied by Club Foot Orchestra; Ana Moura; Chick Corea/Bobby McFerrin/Jack DeJohnette; Lura; James Moody; Mose Allison; Ernestine Anderson; Lee Konitz; Chano Dominguez, Pablo Ziegler; Cherryholmes; Crosspulse Percussion Ensemble; The Bad Plus, Doctor 3; Lynn Harrell plays Bach Solo Cello Suites; Dianne Reeves; Rosa Passos;

Le Mystère des Voix Bulgares; Miles from India (with Ron Carter, Wallace Roney, Badal Roy, Rudresh Mahanthappa, Pete Cosey); SFJAZZ High School All-Stars with Miguel Zenón; Brad Mehldau Trio; Edward Simon and the Ensemble Venezuela, V Note Ensemble, Aquiles Baez Ensemble; David Sanchez; Patricia Barber, Jessica Williams; Taj Mahal, Keb' Mo'

SFJF 2008: Gilberto Gil; The Derek Trucks Band, Susan Tedeschi; Miles from India; Sweet Honey in the Rock; Mavis Staples; "SFJAZZ Beacon Award" with Rebeca Mauleón and Karl Perazzo, Bobi Cespedes, Orestes Vilató; Randy Newman; Max Raabe and Palast Orchester; Mitch Woods's Big Easy Boogie, Zydeco Flames; Dave Brubeck Quartet; Jimmy Scott, Melody Gardot; Archie Shepp; Cecil Taylor; Eldar, Sophie Milman; Maceo Parker; Marilyn Crispell; Peter Apfelbaum and the New York Hieroglyphics; Dave Ellis Quintet, Dayna Stephens Quintet, Mitch Marcus Quintet; Forro in the Dark, DJ Spooky; Ravi Coltrane; Arturo Sandoval; Charlie Haden's Liberation Music Orchestra; Marcin Wasilewski Trio; Toumani Diabaté; Natacha Atlas, Rahim Alhaj; Issac Delgado; "B-3 Summit" with Dr. Lonnie Smith Quartet with Donald Harrison, Godfathers of the Groove (with Reuben Wilson, Grant Green Jr., Bernard Purdie); Wayne Horvitz Gravitas Quartet; Jake Shimabukuro

Spring 2009: John Santos; Albino!, DJ Jeremiah; Jenny Scheinman Quartet; Will Bernard (with John Medeski, Andy Hess, and Stanton Moore); SFJAZZ Collective, Madeleine Peyroux, William Fitzsimmons; The Idan Raichel Project; Branford Marsalis Quartet; Bill Frisell's Disfarmer Project; Ahmad Jamal; Kayhan Kalhor and Brooklyn Rider; John Scofield; Tinariwen; Chris Potter Underground, Ambrose Akinmusire; Adam Theis (premiere of Brass, Bows and Beats); Seun Kuti and Egypt 80; Hugh Masekela; McCoy Tyner Trio with Bobby Hutcherson; Maceo Parker; Joe Louis Walker; Mariza; Mingus Dynasty with John Handy; Karrin Allyson; Michael Feinstein; Céu, Brad Mehldau, solo, and duo with Matt Chamberlain; Richard Bona/Lionel Loueke Duo; Kenny Barron Trio; Kenny Burrell Quartet, Russell Malone Quartet; Glenn Miller Orchestra, Tommy Dorsey Orchestra; "Sacred Space" with James Carter, Roy Hargrove; The Roots; Maria Volonté; Kim Nalley; SFJAZZ High School All-Stars with Eric Harland; Michael Wolff Trio; Hiromi; Linda Tillery and Cultural Heritage Choir; Allen Toussaint Quartet; Goran Bregovic

SFJF 2009: Eric Reed; Omara Portuondo; Jake Shimabukuro; "Benny Goodman Centennial" with Eddie Daniels, Jim Rothermel Swingtet; Omar Sosa Quartet with Tim Eriksen, John Santos Sextet; Melody Gardot; Gonzalo Rubalcaba Quintet; Poncho Sanchez; Henry Butler; Mark Murphy; Gal Costa; Alfredo Rodriguez; Cindy Blackman's Another Lifetime; Ravi Shankar; Yasmin Levy; Dee Dee Bridgewater; "Sacred Space" with Nicholas Payton, Don Byron with Iva Bittova; James Cotton's Superharp with Hubert Sumlin; Marco Benevento, Vinnie Esparza; Marc Cary Focus Trio; Giovanni Allevi, Patrizia Scascitelli; "SFJAZZ Beacon Award" with John Handy and Don Thompson, Terry Clarke, Rob Thomas, Michelle Colucci, Tarika Lewis, Robbie Kwock, Jeff Chambers, Carlos Reyes, Dave Mathews, Deszon Claiborne, Kenny Washington; Trio 3 (Oliver Lake, Reggie Workman, Andrew Cyrille); Jesus Diaz y Su QBA, Scott Amendola vs. Will Blades, Jaz Sawyer and Drum Circle; Esperanza Spalding; Sara Tavares; Pat Martino Trio with Eric Alexander, Larry Goldings Trio; Milton Nascimento; Savion Glover; Carolina Chocolate Drops; Ornette Coleman; John Abercrombie Quartet; Keb' Mo', Solomon Burke

Spring 2010: Issac Delgado; Max Raabe and Palast Orchester; Tinariwen; "Sacred Space" with Joshua Redman; Al Di Meola World Symphonia; SFJAZZ Collective, Kate McGarry; Zakir Hussain's Masters of Percussion; Dianne Reeves; Ladysmith Black Mambazo; Rudresh Mahanthappa; Maceo Parker; Keith Jarrett, solo; Hiromi, Robert Glasper Experiment; Ralph Towner and Paolo Fresu; Tord Gustavsen; Bobby McFerrin; Tomasz Stanko; Pharoah Sanders; Caetano Veloso; Punch Brothers with Chris Thile; Booker T.; Ana Moura; Charles Lloyd; Raul Midón; Charlie Musselwhite; Sex Mob with DJ Olive; Sheila Jordan and Steve Kuhn; Soulive, Wil Blades; Faye Carol, Jamie Davis; Bela Fleck/Zakir Hussain/Edgar Meyer; Regina Carter Quintet, Mads Tolling Quartet; Lou Donaldson; Kurt Elling "Sings Sinatra" with The Count Basie Orchestra; Bill Charlap/Renee Rosnes, Toshiko Akiyoshi/Lew Tabackin; Donny McCaslin Trio; Marcus Miller with Christian Scott; Salif Keita; James Farm (Joshua Redman, Aaron Parks, Eric Harland, Matt Penman)

SFJF 2010: Olodum; Chris Potter Underground; Henry Threadgill's Zooid; Marcus Shelby Orchestra; Nikki Yanofsky; Anat Cohen, Avishai Cohen; Esperanza Spalding; Danilo Perez; Chucho Valdés; Manhattan Transfer; Garaj Mahal; Meklit Hadero; Asleep at the Wheel; Heaven on Earth Quintet (with James Carter, John Medeski); Gretchen Parlato; Yusef Lateef; Taj Mahal, Vieux Farka Touré, Foday Musa Suso; Kenny Barron Trio with David Sanchez; Jon Jang; Ravi Shankar; Stew and the Negro Problem; Steve Lehman Octet; Arturo Sandoval; Nellie McKay; Omara Portuondo; Bitches Brew Revisited; Lila Downs; Natacha Atlas; Ledisi; Roy Haynes; Yellowjackets, Jeff Lorber Fusion; Jose James and Jef Neve; Slavic Soul Party!; Rosanne Cash; Vijay Iyer Trio

Spring 2011: Hugh Masekela; Kenny Werner Quintet with David Sanchez and Randy Brecker; Gerald Clayton Trio; Preservation Hall Jazz Band, San Francisco Bourbon Kings; Marc Ribot accompanies Charlie Chaplin's silent film The Kid; Marcus Roberts Trio; Go Home (with Scott Amendola, Ben Goldberg, Charlie Hunter, Ellery Eskelin); Patricia Barber; Yasmin Levy; Jane Monheit; Adam Theis and the Jazz Mafia String Quartet; Jake Shimabukuro; Irma Thomas; John Santos; Madeleine Peyroux; Max Raabe and Palast Orchester; Assad Brothers; "B-3 Summit" with Barbara Dennerlein, Dr. Lonnie Smith; Dafnis Prieto's Proverb Trio; Ellis Marsalis Quartet; Randy Newman; Buddy Guy, John Németh; John Scofield; Lavay Smith Sings Patsy Cline; Gabriela Montero; Céu; Lionel Loeuke; Eliane Elias; Ambrose Akinmusire; Dianne Reeves; Rickie Lee Jones; Tony Bennett; Steve Tyrell; Rova Saxophone Quartet; Lee Ritenour; "A Night in Treme" with Rebirth Brass Band, Kermit Ruffins, Donald Harrison, Big Sam Williams, Dr. Michael White; Youssou N'Dour, Angélique Kidjo; Nikki Yanofsky; Roy Hargrove and Cedar Walton; Ana Moura, Jazz at Lincoln Center Orchestra with Wynton Marsalis

SFJF 2011: Carmen Souza; Booker T.; Tomasz Stanko; Mimi Fox Trio; Pat Metheny; Vinicius Cantuária; Robert Glasper Trio; Asha Bhosle; Esperanza Spalding; Fernando Otero; Eldar Djangirov; Wayne Shorter Quartet; David Binney; Tiempo Libre; Benny Green; Daniela Mercury; Luciana Souza; Indie Arie, Idan Raichel; McCoy Tyner Trio with Chris Potter and Jose James; Huun Huur Tu; Joshua Redman and Brad Mehldau; Jim Hall; Mose Allison; Goran Bregovic; Javon Jackson (with Mulgrew Miller, Jimmy Cobb, and Nate Reeves); Pomplamoose; Bassekou Kouyate; Savion Glover; Pamela Rose; Dorado Schmitt's Django Reinhardt Festival; Anonymous 4; Ahmad Jamal; Aaron Neville

Spring 2012: Enrico Rava Tribe, John Abercrombie Organ Trio; Chucho Valdés; The Chieftains; Dave Holland Overtone Quartet (with Chris Potter, Jason Moran, Eric Harland); Ladysmith Black Mambazo; "Salute to Toots Thielemans" (with Grégoire Maret, Oscar Castro-Neves, Kenny Werner, and Airto Moreira); James "Blood" Ulmer; Chrisette Michele; Uri Caine Trio; Meklit Hadero; Lizz Wright; Vicente Amigo; Chano Domínguez; "Jazz Beacon Award" with Benny Velarde; Raul Midón; Sierra Maestra; Tin Hat; "Dan Hicks 70th Birthday" with Rickie Lee Jones, Tuck and Patti, Maria Muldaur, Harry Shearer, David Grisman, Jim Kweskin, Ramblin' Jack Elliott; Hermeto Pascoal; Michel Camilo; Anoushka Shankar; Kate McGarry; Bill Frisell "The Great Flood"; Charles Lloyd New Quartet; Paco de Lucía; Third World Love; Eli Degibri, Kevin Hays; 3 Cohens, Gilad Hekselman; Maceo Parker; Rosanne Cash; Cyro Baptista's Banquet of the Spirits; Jane Monheit; Tia Fuller Quartet; Brad Mehldau Trio; Kenny Barron and Mulgrew Miller; Gonzalo Rubalcaba; Tinariwen; "Another Night in Treme" with Dr. John, Soul Rebels, Big Chief Monk Boudreaux, Leo Nocentelli, Ivan Neville; Christian McBride Big Band; Céu

SFJF 2012: Esperanza Spalding; Brecker Brothers Band Reunion (with Randy Brecker, Mike Stern, and Dave Weckl); Miles Smiles (with Wallace Roney, Bill Evans, Robben Ford, Joey DeFrancesco, Darryl Jones, Omar Hakim); Sonny Rollins; "Monk's Birthday" with Barry Harris, Jacky Terrasson, Alfredo Rodriguez; Marcus Miller; Danilo Perez; Jerry and Andy Gonzalez, Elio Villafranca and Arturo Stable; Eliane Elias; Septeto Nacional Ignacio Piñeiro de Cuba; Marc Ribot's Border Music with David Hidalgo; Gilberto Gil; Mary Stallings and Bill Charlap Trio; Tony Malaby's Tamarindo with William Parker and Mark Ferber; Grégoire Maret; Robert Glasper Experiment; Orquesta Aragón; Ornette Coleman; Lavay Smith and Her Red Hot Skillet Lickers; Don Byron New Gospel Quintet; Buika; Dorado Schmitt's Django All-Stars; John Medeski; Arturo Sandoval; The Blind Boys of Alabama

SFJAZZ Staff

Current Staff

James Abernathy, Rusty Aceves, Mount V. Allen III, Jessica Bailey, Allison Blomerth, Tamara Bock, Shanna Bowie, Alexandra Casazza, Lalo Cervantes, Karen Chreston, Stephen Clifford, Paul Contos, Katiti Crawford, Montra Egerton, Halley Elwell, Cecilia Engelhart, Laura Evans, Paulette Galiothe, Carmine Garofalo, TJ Gorton, Lizette Gutierrez, Laura Hamilton, Jennifer Hoffecker, Teddy Hutcherson, Jennifer Kiss, Randall Kline, Marshall Lamm, Brenda Laribee, Glenn Larsen, Henriette Lenssen, Mike Levy, Yasmine Love, Susan Mall, Rebeca Mauleón, Ash Maynor, Megan Mock, Katie Neubauer, Lizzie O'Hara, Claire Phillips, Kelley Pickering, Erin Putnam, Naomi Julia Satake, Barrett Shaver, Holly Skipper, Marion Smallwood, Susannah Stringam, Felice Swapp, Geeta Tate, Tommy To, Jeffery Umetsu, Jenever J. Utsey, Justin Walters, Kerry Faith Weddington, Steven Woo, Dann Zinn

Past Staff

Lauren Adams, Cimeron Ahluwalia, Dorothea Alexander, Eric Allen, Abigail Allt, Rachel Alvarez, Michelle Amador, Adrian Amsems, Alicia Andrews, Sigrid Ann, Aaron Arabian, Carla Ayala, Christina Ayala, Carol Bach-y-Rita, Jon Bailey, Susan Barber, David J. Barrett, Courtney Beck, Christopher Berg, Carolyn Bergamaschi, Jonah Berman, Andre Bernal, Janelle Bernath, Steven Berry, Lexine Bhatia, Donna Blakemore, Egidia Bolini, Richard Borgio, Rachel Bouch, Christopher Bowles, Charles Brack, Sandra Braimah, Brandi Brandes, Dan Brandon, Corie Brizuela, Rebecca Broder, Anthony Brown, Jennifer Bruns, Luciana Ramos Bruscagim, Abel Cabral, Matthew Campbell, Michael Cano, Maureen Carroll, Pat Carroll, Kevin Causey, Chida Chaemchaeng, David Challinor, Anne Chao, Mike Charlasch, Brian Chen, Rob Chen, Jarrett Cherner, Edwin Chin, Cecily Chow, Tiffany Christian, Sam Clover, Marli Cocco, David Coffman, Stacey L. Cohen, Cory Combs, Catherine Conway, Jill Corlew, Christina Coughlin, Diane Curtis, Claire Daenzer, Richard Dailey, Jean Davis, Bruce DeBenedictis, Blanca De La Vega, Francois Depayras, Beth Dickinson, Danielle Dillon, Brendan Downs, Tony Dozier, Uliana Duarte, Ann Dyer, Nikki Edwards, Max Eliot, Dave Ellis, Amber Ellis-Seguine, Breanna Elton, Leah Elton, Sarah Engelman, Patricia Evans, Rick Evans, Warren Evans, Audrey Faine, Viki Faktor, Mark Follman, Susie Fong, Christine Ford, Tricia Foster, Drew Foxman, Denise Fraga, Lori Franz, Bill Fraser, Andrea Freedman, Stefanee Freedman, Sallyanne French, Nicole Frydman, Gautam Ganeshan, Cheri Garamendi, Scott Garrison, Linda Saulsby Gaston, Linda Gentile, Laura Giannatempo, Clint Gilbert, Ruth Goldfine, Tatijana Goreta, Christopher Goves, KT Graham, Rebecca Graham, Michael "Geese" Graphix, Jean Greendyke, Judson Gregory, Linda Gruber, Hannah Guggenheim, Anastasia Hacopian, Mark Hagen, John Hamilton, Jeremy Hamm, Daniel Han, Carolyn Hanrahan, Noelle Hanrahan, David Hargis, Jonas Hedegard, Thea Heinz, Andy Heller, Tom Heng, Deborah Hersh, Alberto Hirota, Paula Hobson-Coard, Fred Hoff, Emma Lou Huckabay, Marika Hughes, Chris Huie, Kirsten Hutchinson, Bokyung Hwang, Karen Hyun, Joyce Imbesi, Omar Ivy, Megan Jacobs, Michael Jacobs, Vera Jaye, Colby Jensen, Rebecca Jensen, Fred Johnson, Phyllis Jones, Dorothy Joo, Abo Jose, Jennifer Joyce, Lon Kaisar, Karina Kamali'i, Chandra Karp, Cory Karpin, Holly Kaslewicz, Jerry Katz, Sam Kaufman, Johanna Keith, Lisa Kellman, Amy Knipe, Alex Kogan, Joshua Price

Kol, Lina Konstantinovici, Corey Krehel, Michael Lacina, Ondine Landa, Kate Lange, Dana Lau, Atticus Leat, Marjorie Lefcowitz, Aaron Levin, Alessandra Liberman, Scott Lietzke, David Lilley, Brian Maclaren, Susan Main, Gabriel Marquez, Brian Mason, Dmitri Matheny, Diane Maxwell, James McCaffry, Crystal McElhiney, Cindy McHale, JoAnn McStravick, Shilla Mehrafshani, Hilda Méndez, Jole Bowman Mendoza, Miguel Mendoza, John Miles, David Miller, Joan Miro, Will Mitchell, Yasuo Monno, Ricardo Montalvo, Ryan Morgan, Susanna Mu, Greg Muck, Amy Mueller, LaReva Myles, John Nahigian, David Nakayama, Justin Neal, Larry Neff, Micaela Nerguizian, Howard Nett, Joseph Newkirk, Vân Nguyen, Paul Nicolas, Denise Notzon, Jean-Pierre Nussbaumer, Melissa O'Connell, Zachariah O'hora, Toni Ong, Jennifer Oxley, Deborah Pardes, Amber Pennington, John Pfeifer, Matthew Pham, Andrea Pico, Margaret R. Pico, Cheryl Pierce, Tammy Pioch, Michael Pistorio, Zack Pitt-Smith, Cristiana F.V. Pontes, Joanne S. Porter, Andrea Poulos, Cory Powers, Grace Prasad, Tim Pritchard, Caterina Prochilo, Howard Quinn, Daniella Ragge, Luciana Ragoni, Dennis Rathnaw, Shirley Read-Jahn, Joshua Redman, Tracy Reid, Jerry Reimann, Heather Reisz, Timothy Reynolds, Geovani Ribeiro, Brad Rickman, Jack Riordan, Griff Rollefson, Ann Root, Sarah Rothstein, Charles Rubinoff, Eleanor Ruckman, Joe Salerno, John Santos, Tim Sarraille, Allison Satchell, Daniel Savio, Shirleen Schermerhorn, Bernard Schertzer, Crystal Schimpf, Svend Schjoerring, Jennifer Schwartz, Cubby Sedgwick, Robin Seltzer, Ronnie Shapiro, Mark Shattuck, Laura Shaw, Victoria Shelton, Rowan Sherwood, George Shuai, Michael Shunk, Josh Shuster-Lefkowitz, Estevan Sifuentes, Karina Simpson, Stephanie Simpson, Ann Singer, Suzanna Smith, Ursula Smith, Zinaida Soin, Charles Solari, Maria Sousa, Bud Spangler, Peggy Spaugh, Dianthe "Dee" Spencer, Fred Spitz, Roger Springer, Alex Stefani, Amy Stewart, Kimberly Stewart, Mineh Stewart, Elysia Strauss, Hiromi Suzuki, Robert Sweibel, Jennifer Taher, Cynthia Taylor, DeAndre Taylor, Sasha Terris-Maes, Rob Tocalino, Dipak Topiwala, Lori Ubell, Angela Valley, Francis Van Schooten, Daki Venetoullis, Jason Venetoullis, Dorian Venza, Sean Vigneau-Britt, Antea von Henneberg, Villy Wang, Charles Ward, Rick Warren, Lisa Warrick, Tyrone Watkins, Paul Weinstein, Shenandoah Weiss, Preston West, Mark Westlund, Mike Whelan, Laurie Will, Deanna Williams, Keith Williams, Alex Willis, Robin Wilson, Tony Wilson, Ray Winans, Alex Wolfe, Chris Wood, Jordan Wright, Jane Yau, Isabel Yrigoyen

Index

Page numbers in italics indicate photos.